Disaster Preparedness and the United Nations

(Pergamon Policy Studies—34)

Pergamon Policy Studies on Socio-Economic Development

Published for UNITAR

PERGAMON
POLICY
STUDIES

ON SOCIO-ECONOMIC
DEVELOPMENT

Disaster Preparedness and the United Nations

Advance Planning for Disaster Relief

Barbara J. Brown

Published for UNITAR

Pergamon Press
NEW YORK • OXFORD • TORONTO • SYDNEY • FRANKFURT • PARIS

Pergamon Press Offices:

U.S.A.   Pergamon Press Inc., Maxwell House, Fairview Park, Elmsford, New York 10523, U.S.A.

U.K.   Pergamon Press Ltd., Headington Hill Hall, Oxford OX3 0BW, England

CANADA   Pergamon of Canada, Ltd., 150 Consumers Road, Willowdale, Ontario M2J, 1P9, Canada

AUSTRALIA   Pergamon Press (Aust) Pty. Ltd., P O Box 544, Potts Point, NSW 2011, Australia

FRANCE   Pergamon Press SARL, 24 rue des Ecoles, 75240 Paris, Cedex 05, France

FEDERAL REPUBLIC Pergamon Press GmbH, 6242 Kronberg/Taunus,
OF GERMANY   Pferdstrasse 1, Federal Republic of Germany

Library of Congress Cataloging in Publication Data

Brown, Barbara Jean, 1950-
 Disaster preparedness.

 (Pergamon policy studies)
 Bibliography: p.
 Includes index.
 1. Disaster relief—Planning. 2. Disaster
relief. 3. United Nations. I. Title.
HV553.B76 1979   363.3'4   79-179
ISBN 0-08-022486-5

Printed in the United States of America

Contents

List of Figures and Tables

Foreword

The international community has noted with growing concern the impact of natural disasters on human life and property, particularly in the developing countries. The United Nations and its specialized agencies have always had an interest in and commitment to disaster relief. In recent years the role of the United Nations in disaster relief has expanded considerably. There are now disaster relief, preparedness, prevention and mitigation programs being carried out by a variety of United Nations organizations and agencies with the United Nations Disaster Relief Coordinator playing a central role. The question of whether or not traditional arrangements for providing international disaster relief are still adequate has been a recurrent topic in the deliberative forums of the United Nations, as well as in the governing bodies of the specialized agencies. In the present climate of change and debate, all organizations concerned are reviewing their policies and methods of operation, and even some of their fundamental assumptions about their roles in disaster assistance.

This study, by Dr. Barbara J. Brown, examines the roles and relationships of a number of United Nations programs in the area of disaster relief and preparedness. The existing literature devoted to disaster research reveals very little about the complexities of organizational functioning during a disaster, particularly at the international level. The author has focused her analysis and proposals on United Nations disaster preparedness programs in an effort to produce a practical reference guide of use to scholars as well as to international program administrators. She has drawn upon archives and documents from the collections of the United Nations and several specialized agencies. Additional data were obtained from interviews with administrators of national disaster preparedness programs in developing countries and officials of the United Nations.

Within the framework of the definition of disaster preparedness as it relates to the United Nations, Dr. Brown focuses the study on two subjects: the respective roles of several United Nations agencies and programs involved in disaster-related assistance, and the need for disaster preparedness in the most disaster-prone developing countries. There is a brief introductory look at the relationship between disasters and development, in which the necessity of viewing natural disasters as a problem of development becomes clear, and a description of the international disaster relief system that takes account of the role of the United Nations within this system.

The major focus of the study examines the current disaster preparedness activities of the United Nations from two perspectives: the programs designed to improve the preparedness posture of disaster-prone developing countries, and the programs designed to improve the disaster relief capabilities of the organizations. The internal organizational arrangements of the agencies are examined to determine to what extent these arrangements contribute to or work against increased involvement in disaster preparedness. The main obstacles to increased involvement are discussed as well as various strategies for overcoming them.

In accordance with United Nations Institute for Training and Research (UNITAR) practice, an earlier draft of this study was reviewed by a panel of diplomats, officials of the United Nations, representatives of nongovernmental organizations, and scholars. The study benefited greatly from their observations and suggestions and the written comments submitted by other experts. It is hoped that the ideas and analyses contained in the study will serve the practical needs of those involved in development programming.

The author, Dr. Barbara J. Brown, was a Research Associate in the Department of Research, UNITAR. Her work was carried out with the help of a grant from the Rockefeller Foundation for which UNITAR is grateful.

The views and conclusions presented in this study are the responsibility of the author and do not necessarily reflect the opinions of the Board of Trustess or officials of UNITAR or of the Rockefeller Foundation. While UNITAR takes no position on the views expressed by the authors of its studies, it does assume responsibility for determining whether a study merits publication and dissemination.

We are pleased to publish this UNITAR study by Dr. Brown.

Davidson Nicol
Under-Secretary General
Executive Director, UNITAR
September 1978

Acknowledgments

The cooperation and support of the United Nations Institute for Training and Research (UNITAR) is greatly appreciated. A special thank-you is extended to Dr. Davidson Nicol, Executive Director of UNITAR, and Dr. Robert Jordan, Director of Research, who both gave generously of their time and shared some valuable insights into some of the problems facing the United Nations.

The author is indebted to a great number of United Nations officials, too numerous to mention individually, who gave valuable advice and counsel regarding their organizations' activities in disaster preparedness. Several officials at the League of Red Cross Societies also contributed generously in the preparation of this report.

A final thank-you to Ms. Helen E. Coutroulos and Ms. Remedios D. De Jesus for their efficient assistance in typing the manuscript.

Members of Panel

Angelo R. Cinti	American Red Cross
Mamadou Dagra	Niger Mission to the United Nations
Virendra Dayal	Office of the United Nations High Commissioner for Refugees
Claude de Ville de Goyet	Pan American Health Organization/World Health Organization
Clermonde Dominice	International Committee of the Red Cross
Anna Maria Jaguaribe	United Nations Development Program
A. Razzaque Khan	Bangladesh Mission to the United Nations
Ilhan Lutem	Office of the United Nations Disaster Relief Coordinator
S.A. Malafatopoulos	World Health Organization
Leon Marion	American Council of Voluntary Agencies for Foreign Service
Richard Pordes	United Nations Children's Fund
Mr. Steven E. Ramondt	Netherlands Mission to the United Nations
Michael Reilly	American Red Cross
Timothy Rothermel	United Nations Development Programme
Tayyab Siddiqui	Pakistan Mission to the United Nations
Lynn Stephens	Carnegie Endowment for International Peace
Ibrahim Sy	Senegal Mission to the United Nations
Gilda E. Varrati	United States Mission to the United Nations

Josue Villa	Philippine Mission to the United Nations
Robert Walker	United Nations Children's Fund
Frederick H. Weibgen	Food and Agriculture Organization
Charles H. Weitz	Food and Agriculture Organization

UNITAR

Davidson Nicol	Executive Director
Robert S. Jordan	Director of Research
Alexandre Mironov	Deputy Director of Research
John de Gara	Special Fellow
Barbara J. Brown	Research Associate

Glossary of Terms

In the varied activities associated with disasters, be it relief, prevention, or preparedness, a number of terms have entered into common usage. In order to avoid confusion and in the interests of uniformity, the meanings suggested by the Office of the United Nations Disaster Relief Coordinator (UNDRO) are used throughout this study.

PREPAREDNESS

Disaster preparedness may be described as action designed to minimize loss of life and damage, and to organize and facilitate timely and effective rescue, relief and rehabilitation in cases of disaster.

Preparedness is supported by the necessary legislation and means a readiness to cope with disaster situations or similar emergencies that cannot be avoided. Preparedness is concerned with forecasting and warning; education and training of the population; organization for and management of disaster situations, including preparation of operational plans, training of relief groups, stockpiling of supplies, and earmarking of the necessary funds.

PREVENTION

Disaster prevention may be described as measures designed to prevent natural phenomena from causing or resulting in disaster or other related emergency situations.

Prevention concerns the formulation and implementation of long-range policies and programs to prevent or eliminate the occurrence of disasters. On the basis of vulnerability analyses of all risks, prevention includes legislation and regulatory measures, principally in the fields of physical and urban planning, public works, and building.

Glossary of Acronyms

ACABO	Advisory Committee on Administration and Budgetary Questions
COPUOS	Committee on the Peaceful Uses of Outer Space
ECOSOC	Economic and Social Council
EEC	European Economic Community
ECLA	Economic Commission for Latin America
ESCAP	Economic and Social Commission for Asia and the Pacific
FAO	Food and Agriculture Organization
IAEA	International Atomic Energy Agency
IBRD	The World Bank
ICEM	Intergovernmental Committee for European Migration
ICRC	International Committee of the Red Cross
ICVA	International Council of Voluntary Agencies
IDA	International Development Association
IFC	International Finance Corporation
IMF	International Monetary Fund
ILO	International Labor Organization
ITU	International Telecommunications Union
LORCS	League of Red Cross Societies
OAU	Organization for African Unity
OECD	Organization for Economic Cooperation and Development
OSRO	FAO Office for Special Relief Operations (formerly Office for Sahelian Relief Operations)
PAHO	Pan American Health Organization
SPEC	South Pacific Bureau for Economic Cooperation
UNCTAD	United Nations Conference on Trade and Development
UNDP	United Nations Development Program
UNDRO	Office of the United Nations Disaster Relief Coordinator
UNEP	United Nations Environment Program

UNESCO   United Nations Educational, Scientific and Cultural
              Organization
UNHCR   Office of the United Nations High Commissioner for
              Refugees
UNICEF   United Nations Children's Fund
UNIDO   United Nations Industrial Development Organization
UNSO   United Nations Sahelian Office
WFP   World Food Program
WHO   World Health Organization
WMO   World Meteorological Organization

1 Dateline Disaster

IRAN - March 23, 1977...

An earthquake struck southern Iran today and the government radio said 60 persons had been killed in villages near the Persian Gulf. Scenes of panic were reported as some buildings were damaged by tremors which registered 7 on the Richter scale. Iran lies in an earthquake belt and Bandar Abbas has been affected in the past.(1)

HAITI - May 17, 1977...

The worst of three years of sparse rainfall has brought hundreds of thousands of Haitians to the brink of starvation, relief officials say. "What happened this year is that some rural people on the borderline of starvation started to starve," a foreign official said....A major international relief effort is underway.(2)

ZAIRE - June 8, 1977...

Three farming villages and as many farmers in a remote region of Zaire were incinerated early this year when a molten lake of lava rushed down the sides of a volcano that had not erupted since 1928....The lava flow stopped three miles from Goma, a city of 65,000 population.(3)

INDIA - November 22, 1977...

   The Government began a major relief effort
today as the official estimate of deaths from the
state of Andhra Pradesh Saturday grew to
10,000....The cyclone - the Indian Ocean equivalent
of a hurricane - has been described as the worst
natural disaster in this country since 35,000 people
died in a tidal wave in 1864. At this time every
year, coastal areas along the Bay of Bengal face
the anger of cyclones....Despite early warning of
the cyclone's approach, the people and local
government officials took hardly any preventive
steps. (4)

Disasters happen everywhere. An earthquake in Iran, a
drought in Haiti, a volcanic eruption in Zaire or a cyclone in
India - disaster events are not unique but occur with some
degree of repetition or regularity over time, bringing death
and destruction to millions of people around the world.
   Disaster may be the second major human problem after
war, in terms of monetary damage and number of people killed
or affected. It is difficult to assess the precise impact of
disasters on the countries involved, but one estimate suggests
that in the decade 1964 to 1974, the world suffered more than
400 major natural disasters, resulting in 3.5 million deaths,
over 400 million people affected and $11 billion in damage.
During that same period, international relief donors contributed $2.8 billion. (5) Attaching numerical value to the
destruction disasters can bring does not reveal the real
significance of the disaster problem. While the initial impact
of a disaster may last only a few seconds, as in the case of an
earthquake, the effect of a disaster upon individual and
community life is immeasurable and may last for generations.
   Major disaster relief organizations are continually required
to deal with several operations simultaneously. Adding to the
complexity of every relief operation is the fact that hundreds
of different organizations may be involved in a single disaster
assistance operation.
   The United Nations and its specialized agencies play a
key role in most international disaster relief operations. Since
1945 and the creation of the United Nations and its specialized
agencies, there has been an interest in and commitment to
disaster relief within international organizations. In terms of
material resources, the efforts of these agencies can only be
viewed as supplemental to those of bilateral government donors.
However, throughout the years, the role of the United Nations
system in disaster relief has served increasingly important
functions. With representatives in over one hundred devel-

oping countries, the commitment of the United Nations to development assistance has produced experienced personnel in many disaster-prone areas and has provided close contact wth local government officials. Expertise in such areas as maternal and child care, public health, transportation and communications, agriculture, and food has provided the opportunity for many governments to direct their disaster relief assistance through one of the United Nations organizations.

The subject of disaster assistance has emerged as a critical issue within the United Nations. In the past few years, the question of whether or not traditional approaches and institutional arrangements for providing international disaster relief are still adequate has been a recurrent topic in the United Nations Economic and Social Council (ECOSOC) and the General Assembly, as well as in the governing bodies of several organizations such as the United Nations Children's Fund (UNICEF), the World Health Organization (WHO), and the Food and Agriculture Organization (FAO).

From these discussions certain conclusions about disaster assistance have emerged.

1) Disasters are not isolated incidents but development problems requiring planned, coordinated and long-term responses.
2) While disaster relief is necessary, it should not remain the only United Nations strategy for combating disaster.
3) Greater attention should be paid to disaster preparedness and disaster prevention programs.

In the present climate of change and debate over the scope of United Nations activities in disaster relief, preparedness and prevention, all organizations concerned are reviewing their policies and methods of operation and even some of their fundamental assumptions about their roles in disaster preparedness and prevention.

NATURE AND PURPOSE OF THE STUDY

The primary purpose of this research is to investigate the potential benefits and problems involved in formulating national disaster preparedness plans in disaster-prone developing countries, and some possible ways in which the United Nations agencies can more effectively promote programs of disaster preparedness. The focus will be on the respective roles of several United Nations agencies and programs involved and the potential they exhibit for increased involvement in disaster preparedness. Although the nature of each organization's efforts in disaster relief will be reviewed, the perspective of the study is oriented toward preparedness activities. One of the goals of this research is to determine to what extent the present internal organizational arrangements of those agencies involved in disaster relief contribute to or work against increased involvement in disaster preparedness. The main obstacles to increased United Nations involvement will be discussed as well as various strategies for overcoming these problems.

Another aspect of this study concerns the disaster-prone developing countries of the world, their needs for disaster preparedness, and their difficulties in implementing preparedness programs. The objectives of this particular examination are:

1) To study the state of disaster preparedness in some less developed disaster-prone countries;
2) To identify and analyze the main areas of deficiency;
3) To study the possible ways of improving the state of disaster preparedness in these developing countries; and
4) To assess the availability of United Nations resources with a view to formulating a practical approach for increased involvement in funding preparedness programs.

The general importance of preparedness programs relative to other uses of development assistance will be examined. The question will be raised whether the United Nations is using its advisory role as effectively as it could to stimulate governments to establish preparedness programs. Some suggestions will be offered which may lead to more rapid development of disaster plans and organizations in the most needy countries.

The study is not intended to examine in detail the problems facing the United Nations in disaster relief or to present an account of past relief operations, but rather to be a guide to the subject of disaster preparedness and the role the United Nations could play.

The remainder of this chapter contains a brief look at the relationship between disasters and development. Chapter 2 describes the international disaster relief system, summarizes the role of the United Nations within this system, and analyzes the main problems encountered in relief operations. Chapter 3 deals with the subject of disaster preparedness, the current state of preparedness planning in disaster-prone developing countries, and the critical issues facing governments which want to institute such planning. Chapter 4 examines the current activities of the United Nations with regard to disaster preparedness and analyzes the prospects for increased involvement in the future. Chapter 5 contains concluding remarks.

DISASTERS AND DEVELOPMENT

The term "disaster" is a descriptive term of administrative origin which has been applied to any event causing loss or suffering on a scale sufficient to warrant an extraordinary response from outside the affected area or community.(6) In determining whether or not an event is to be considered a disaster, the word has been used in a variety of ways. For example, disaster often refers to the disaster agent, such as a hurricane, earthquake, or flood. A second use of the term refers to the physical impact which the agent has, such as damage to property or loss of life. Disaster also has a meaning dependent upon an evaluation of the agent. Damage may be evaluated as disastrous in one area but not in another. This depends upon the relative vulnerability of the community. Finally, disaster can mean the socioeconomic disruption created by the physical event.(7)

A wide variety of forces can cause disasters. These forces may be either natural or man-made, or a combination of both. Within the category of man-made disasters, there are a variety of conditions resulting in disaster:

a) Civil disturbances; riots and demonstrations;
b) Warfare: conventional, nuclear, biological, chemical, guerilla warfare, including terrorism;
c) Refugees: forced movements of large numbers of people, usually across frontiers; and
d) Accidents: transportation accidents, collapse of buildings, dams, etc., mine disasters, and technological failures such as pollution, chemical leaks, or nuclear accidents.

Within the category of natural disasters, there is also a variety of forces that may result in disaster:

a) Meteorological disasters: storms (cyclones, hailstorms, hurricanes, tornadoes, typhoons and snowstorms), cold spells, heat waves and droughts (possibly causing famine);
b) Topological disasters: earthquakes, avalanches, landslides, and floods; and
c) Biological disasters: insect swarms (e.g., locusts) and epidemics of communicable diseases.(8)

The division between natural and man-made is, to some
extent, an oversimplification, as many disasters are actually
caused by more than one or a combination of both types of
forces. For example, flooding could be caused by a heavy
rainstorm, the bombing of a dike, or the collapse of a dam. A
drought could be the result of adverse meteorological conditions, but could become a disaster because of man's policies
of overgrazing or deforestation. In addition, natural events
only become disasters when they directly affect man's habitat.
It must also be pointed out that some types of disasters
are followed by others. For example, a meteorological disaster
like a cyclone can be followed by a topological disaster like a
flood, which may eventually result in a biological disaster like
an epidemic of cholera. In the man-made category, a war,
civil disturbance or accident may result in a refugee problem.
Some of the worst disasters have been caused by the
cumulative effects of several of these factors. For example, in
November 1970, a cyclone followed by one of the worst tidal
waves in history struck the coastal region of East Pakistan
(now Bangladesh) in the Bay of Bengal. It is estimated that
500,000 died, most of the livestock drowned, all the crops
were destoyed, and soil and water were polluted. The United
Nations coordinated a massive international relief effort in
Dacca. The occurrence of this natural disaster came at a time
of civil strife, and four months later the new state of
Bangladesh was established. The civil disturbances forced ten
million people to flee to India, creating another relief operation
in Calcutta. The combined natural and man-made disasters
resulted in one of the biggest relief operations since World War
II. It has been estimated that the entire population of
Bangladesh, some 75 million people, was affected and the cost
of the relief operation reached over $1,318,850,000.(9)
It is difficult to predict precisely where and when a
man-made disaster will occur, and therefore, it is more difficult to prepare for one. It is possible, however, with
varying degrees of accuracy, to predict the occurrence of a
natural disaster. Natural disasters, which are the primary
concern of this study, usually occur within two general
geographical paths. One of these "disaster paths" runs along
the Mediterranean to the Middle East, Afghanistan, Pakistan,
India, Bangladesh down to Indonesia and then north to Japan.
Within this path lies an earthquake-prone belt from Iran
through Turkey and Greece to Yugoslavia, and a cyclone- and
typhoon-prone area around the South China Sea and the Bay
of Bengal. The second disaster path lies along the Andes
through the Caribbean and the Gulf of Mexico. Within this
path lies an earthquake-prone belt down the west coast of the
Americas and a hurricane-prone, earthquake-prone belt of the
Caribbean and Gulf areas.
What is most important to realize about natural disasters

is that they are not isolated, unique, or extraordinary events. In many countries there are disaster subcultures which regularly and continually experience these events. Most recent research has viewed the disaster event as an extreme manifestation of a continuous state of hazard:

> It is essential...to view disaster as an extreme within a series of non-extreme events – an extension of everyday life. Where the latter is as important to an understanding of disaster as the manifestation itself.(10)

The view that the potential for disaster or disaster vulnerability exists prior to the natural event shifts the entire focus upon the problem from the short-term disaster relief approach to the longer-term development approach. The short-term view sees disasters as inevitable and relief as the remedy. The longer-term perspective sees disaster as an interaction of a combination of political, social, economic, and environmental forces which work to "undermine the ability of a system to cope with new stresses."(11) As one author has expressed it,

> The interaction of these factors, which are generally long-term in nature, creates the conditions for disaster....The conditions for disaster can exist for a long period of time before catastrophe strikes. Very often it is the impact of some natural phenomenon which overloads the system. It is the close association between breakdown and natural phenomena which gives rise to the tendency to describe events as "natural" disasters.(12)

Large regions of the world are vulnerable to natural disasters and are becoming increasingly vulnerable. Table 1.1 illustrates the frequency of United Nations disaster relief operations in different regions of the developing world since 1963. There are almost twice as many relief operations in Africa as there are in any other region, with Asia and the Pacific placing second among disaster-prone regions. Other data for a 20-year period indicate a much greater number of disasters for the Asian region but an almost equal average loss of life per disaster as in Africa. Table 1.2 illustrates the comparative vulnerability of the developing world to disasters in terms of loss of life. Asia lost over 32 times as many people per disaster than did North America with a relatively comparable number of disasters recorded. Africa lost over 3 times as many people as Australasia with a comparable number of disasters.

Table 1.1.   United Nations Disaster Relief Operations:
1963-1977.

Region	World Food Programs (1963-1972)	Office of the United Nations Disaster Relief Coordinator (1972-1977)	Total
Africa (south of the Sahara)	64	28	92
North Africa and Near East	34	14	48
Asia and Pacific	32	25	57
Latin America and Caribbean	23	20	43
Europe	6	7	13
Total	159	94	253

Source: United Nations, General Assembly, Thirtieth Session,
May   1975,   Office of the United Nations Disaster Relief Coordinator: Report of the Secretary-General (A/10079); Thirty-
first Session, May 1976 (A/31/88); Thirty-second Session, May
1977 (A/32/64); Thirty-second session, November 25, 1977
(A/C. 5/32/49).

Table 1.2. Average Loss of Life per Disaster
Impact by Continent

Continent	Lives Lost	Number of Disasters	Average Loss of Life per Disaster Event
North America	7,965	210	37
Central America and Caribbean	14,820	49	302
South America	15,670	45	348
Africa	18,105	17	1,065
Europe (excluding USSR)	19,575	85	230
Asia (excluding USSR)	361,410	297	1,216
Australasia	4,310	13	332

Source: L. Sheehan and K. Hewitt, "A Pilot Survey of Global Natural Disasters of the Past Twenty Years," Natural Hazard Research Working Paper No. 11 (Boulder: University of Colorado, Department of Behavioral Science, 1969).

Population growth, lack of planning in human settlements, declining food production, and rising energy and food costs have all contributed to making some areas of the developing world increasingly susceptible to natural disasters. It does not appear that this situation will significantly improve in the near future. In fact, the term "megadisasters" has been coined to describe the disasters of the 1980s, when population growth and the concentration of humanity in disaster-prone areas will produce catastrophes greater than any the world has previously known(13).

A study done by the United Nations Association of the United States of America cites statistics which indicate that the expected population growth in the developing world between 1975 and 1990 will be 41 percent and in the least developed and most disaster-prone countries the growth is expected to be 50 percent.(14) With this increase in population there is also an increase in the concentration of populations in areas vulnerable to natural disasters.

Accompanying the problem of population growth is the problem of food availability. A recent report by the Food and Agriculture Organization (FAO) states that world food production would rise by only 1.5 percent in 1977, while population growth was estimated at 2 percent.(15) Not only do these statistics have implications for the vulnerability of the developing world to famine, they also have implications for the continuation of large-scale disaster relief, since approximately 80 percent of all relief provided in natural disasters is food.(16)

Since 1972, the developing countries have been confronted with a series of international economic developments which have made them especially vulnerable to disasters: a succession of bad harvests in 1972 and 1974, recurrent crises in international money and foreign exchange markets since mid-1971, rapid acceleration of inflation in industrialized countries until mid-1975, and sharp increases in oil prices. These developments have had significant repercussions on the economies of almost all countries, but the poorest of the developing countries have been hit the hardest because of their low per capita incomes, lack of foreign exchange, and incapacity to recover from their disaster losses.

In addition to population growth, unplanned human settlements, a relative decline in food production, and rising energy costs, some evidence tends to support the view that more disasters are occurring than ever before (Table 1.3).

During the four-year period from 1968 to 1971, there appears to be a significant increase in the average number of disasters per year as compared with the 52-year period from 1919 to 1971. Much of this increase in later years can be attributed to better reporting. However, other data reveal that, in addition to this increase, there has been an increase in large-scale disasters and an increase in the number of deaths per year per million population (Figure 1.1). These data suggest an increased vulnerability on the part of the developing world to natural disasters.

Although two-thirds of the world's population live in developing countries, it has been estimated that 95 percent of the disaster-related deaths occur in these countries. In contrast to the exceptional regional differences in death rates indicated in Table 1.2, losses from natural disasters are closely correlated to world income distribution. As much as three-fourths of the global disaster losses occur in the developed countries, but the proportional number of losses in terms of percentage of the gross national product (GNP) is much higher in the developing countries.(17)

Table 1.3.   Disaster Average by Type per Year,
1919-1971

Type	1919-1971	1968-1971	Percent Increase
Cyclone, hurricane, etc.	0.62	1.75	182.26
Drought	0.13	1.25	861.50
Earthquake	1.30	2.00	53.80
Epidemic	0.19	0.50	163.60
Flood	2.70	6.75	150.00
Volcanic Eruption*	0.06	0.25	316.60
Famine	0.25	0.50	100.00

*Small sample produces high ranking for volcanic eruptions.

Source: A. Baird, P. O'Keefe, K. Westgate, and B. Wisner, "Towards an Explanation and Reduction of Disaster Proneness," Occasional Paper No. 11, University of Bradford Disaster Research Unit, Bradford, Yorkshire, United Kingdom, 1975, p. 25.

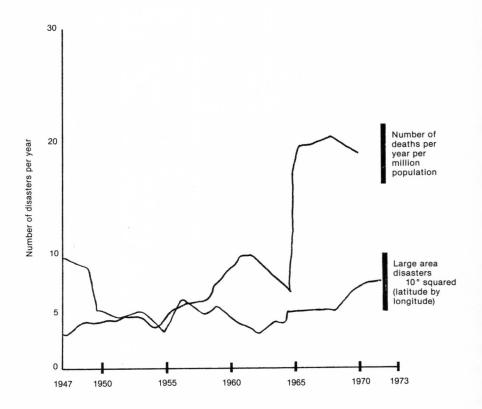

Fig. 1.1.   Global Disasters, 1947–1973
(Five-Year Moving Average)

Source: J.   Devorkin,   "Global   Trends   in   Natural   Disasters
1947–1973."   Natural   Hazard   Research   Working   Paper   No.   26,
Boulder: University   of   Colorado,   Department   of   Behavioral
Science, 1977.

Natural disasters continue to affect economic and social progress years after the disaster has occurred. "In terms of percentage of gross national product, the losses caused by disasters in the disaster-prone developing countries more than cancel out any real economic growth."(18) Living under conditions of marginal existence, developing countries often lack the resources and infrastructure to cope with the additional impact of natural disasters. It has been estimated, for example, that in the five countries of the Central American Common Market, disaster damage has averaged 2.3 percent of the gross domestic product (GDP) in the 15-year period from 1960 to 1974, but it is difficult to obtain accurate assessments of the real costs and overall impact of disasters for most disaster-prone developing countries. Since the countries have a population growth rate of about 3 percent a year, an economic growth rate of at least 5.3 percent must be attained in order to avoid an annual decline.(19) With a 2.3 percent decline in GDP due to disasters, the net growth rate only equals the population growth rate, and therefore results in an annual decline in economic growth. This fact clearly illustrates that disasters should be viewed as a problem of development.

An example of the prolonged effects of disaster is evidenced by the Sahelian drought. About 12 million people were seriously affected, with some seven million dependent on food aid by 1974. The number of deaths was probably between 100,000 and 200,000, including a disproportionate number of children and old people. Many children, weakened by malnutrition, succumbed to measles. This disease, which can be deadly in Africa, had been almost eradicated a few years earlier in a massive campaign against measles and smallpox, but the youngest children had not been vaccinated. One may perceive the impact of the drought on the long-term health of the area's inhabitants as more serious than the immediate deaths resulting from famine. Because prolonged malnutrition reduces resistance to disease, medical authorities predict markedly higher death rates for at least the next five years. Inadequate nutrition in early childhood also can result in some degree of mental retardation.

There is no evidence to suggest that the frequency of natural disasters will alter significantly in the immediate future. But if current trends of high population growth and the movement toward increased urbanization and settlement in disaster-prone areas continue, the effect of these trends will become far more serious.

2 An Overview of the International Disaster Relief System

Until very recently, most international activity related to disasters has been in the form of relief to the victims after the disaster has occurred. Because the actual and potential consequences of disasters are so serious and increasingly global in scale, relief measures and post-disaster actions have not proven to be sufficient in combating the problem. There have been a number of changes in the ways in which the international disaster relief system operates. This discussion will summarize some of these changes and some of the critical problems still prevalent in disaster relief operations.

The international disaster relief "system" is, in many instances, a "non-system." The hundreds of multilateral, bilateral and private organizations that may serve as donors in a single relief operation tend to act independently of each other and to exchange very little information during the course of their relief activities. Although the total number of potential disaster relief donors can be quite large, the actual number of serious donors is, in fact, quite small. Among those donors which are repeatedly involved in almost every major relief operation, the exchange of information is good, although it can be improved. The "non-system" is due, in large measure, to individual ad hoc groups or inexperienced organizations which send small amounts of supplies which, when aggregated, cause difficulties in storage, sorting or distribution. The major actors in the international relief system can be grouped into four general categories: governments, international organizations, voluntary agencies and the international media. Several of these actors have been reviewing their roles and new approaches and institutional relationships have emerged.

THE ROLE OF GOVERNMENTS

The largest amount of relief assistance is usually provided by the government and by the people of the disaster-stricken country. Thus, the distinction that is often made between disaster relief "recipients" and "donors" is both unfortunate and artificial. A staff member of the United States Agency for International Development estimates that "local" assistance in major international disasters in the eleven years from 1965 to 1976 was almost twice that of all the international disaster assistance provided.(1) Somehow, the local and national sense of community and the kaleidoscopic international response must merge into an effort of mutual cooperation to alleviate human suffering.

The government of the disaster-stricken country inevitably bears the primary responsibility for the administration of relief operations. The responsibility for executing the various sectors of the relief program is usually transferred to the appropriate ministries. In the pre-disaster stage, governments should be assured of access to an early warning system that will provide notice of impending disaster, so that they in turn can warn the threatened population. Once disaster strikes, a variety of government ministries are usually the source of initial damage and casualty estimates as well as assessments of needed material assistance and personnel support for the relief operation. If it is determined that the needs of disaster victims cannot be met locally, then the government should initiate requests for assistance, and should coordinate these requests to external donors in order to avoid duplication or omission. Internal distribution of relief supplies is also a national responsibility; international organizations, voluntary agencies, and foreign government missions do not usually have the personnel to distribute supplies on the scale required in a major disaster. Finally, the government of the disaster-stricken country should monitor distribution of supplies, both to keep track of ongoing needs and to report on end use.

The methods used by governments to administer disaster relief vary greatly. While many government institutions may be involved in a disaster relief operation, the executive office is the final authority directing the effort. Several countries have permanent standing national disaster relief organizations. These organizations usually coordinate the efforts of government and private interests within the country, and, in some cases, may coordinate other international assistance as well. The degree to which interministerial coordination is possible varies greatly, and the extent to which the authority of this hierarchical arrangement is integrated at lower administrative levels is also quite variable. In some cases, the organization exists only in theory and has no disaster plan.

Other governments appoint a particular ministry, usually the military, civil defense organization, or police, to play a primary role in the relief operation. Still others delegate the National Red Cross or Red Crescent Society to provide a focal point for directing or coordinating assistance during the immediate emergency phase. Unfortunately, in some disasters none of these preplanned arrangements apply, and a relief effort must be mounted very quickly and often haphazardly on an ad hoc basis.

Foreign governments provide the largest proportion of disaster relief assistance coming from outside the stricken country. In the Sahelian drought relief operation from 1973 to 1975, 88 percent of total international assistance was provided bilaterally.(2) Just as the in-country arrangements for administering relief operations vary from country to country, so do the procedures of the external contributors. Governments require different information regarding relief needs and even within the same bureaucracy different types of commodities have different reporting requirements. All of this greatly increases the complexity of the relief operation.

In recent years, several donor governments have increased the proportion of their development aid budgets earmarked for disaster relief. Others have changed their administrative structures. The United Kingdom, for example, established a specialized Disaster Unit in 1974 within its Ministry of Overseas Development, a development from an earlier unit in the Foreign and Commonwealth Office, dating from the mid-1960s. Similar units have been set up in the Swedish International Development Authority and the Government of the Federal Republic of Germany. The United States Agency for International Development's Office of Foreign Disaster Assistance is the largest and oldest of these special disaster units. The European Economic Community (EEC) also has a unit for disaster relief assistance. Disaster assistance has also been a topic of discussion within the Development Assistance Committee of the Organization for Economic Cooperation and Development (OECD), a forum normally concerned with longer-term economic and social development programs.

While it is difficult to precisely determine the relative importance of bilateral, multilateral, and voluntary contributions to disaster relief in general, it is important to note that foreign governments, as a group, are the primary contributors in the international disaster relief system.

THE ROLE OF INTERNATIONAL ORGANIZATIONS

The United Nations and its specialized agencies very often play a key role in disaster relief. It has been estimated that in 1975 almost $35 million was spent by the United Nations system on disaster activities (primary relief), $13.5 million was spent by regional development banks (primarily for re-habilitation of disaster-stricken areas), and nearly $2 million by nongovernmental organizations.(3)

There are two broad sets of circumstances in which relief assistance is furnished by the United Nations: 1) when man-made disaster situations are involved, and 2) when emer-gencies arise from natural disasters. When a refugee situation occurs as a result of some man-made disaster (for example, civil disturbances, war, revolution) the Office of the United Nations High Commissioner for Refugees (UNHCR) is usually involved in relief operations. The essential humanitarian tasks under-taken by the High Commissioner for assistance to the victims of man-made disasters are essentially to provide relief as-sistance, voluntary repatriation, assistance in the rehabilitation of those returnees, integration, and resettlement.

In cases where assistance to refugees and displaced persons has called for the combined efforts of several members of the United Nations, the High Commissioner has been designated by the Secretary-General to coordinate such as-sistance, as in the case of assistance to the East Bengali refugees, the South Sudan Operation following the Addis Ababa peace settlement, and the United Nations program for humanitarian aid to displaced persons in Cyprus and Angola.

The primary actors in coordinating United Nations as-sistance in natural disaster relief operations are the Office of the United Nations Disaster Relief Coordinator (UNDRO) in Geneva and the United Nations Development Programme (UNDP) Resident Representative in the disaster-stricken country, who represents UNDRO. UNDRO was created by the United Nations General Assembly in 1971 to provide "an adequate permanent office in the United Nations which shall be the focal point in the United Nations system for disaster relief mat-ters."(4) The mandate included the following responsibilities and areas of activity:

1) To establish and maintain co-operation with all organizations and to make advance arrange-ments for ensuring effective assistance;
2) To mobilize, direct and co-ordinate the relief activities of the United Nations system and to co-ordinate this assistance with that given by other intergovernmental and non-governmental organizations;

3)   To receive disaster relief contributions for
      assistance to be carried out by the United
      Nations system;
4)   To assist the government of a disaster-stricken
      country to assess its needs, and to disseminate
      that information to prospective donors, and to
      serve as a clearinghouse for assistance ex-
      tended or planned;
5)   To promote the study, prevention, control and
      prediction of natural disasters;
6)   To assist in providing advice to governments
      on pre-disaster planning and to draw upon
      United Nations resources for such purposes;
      and
7)   To disseminate information on the improvement
      and establishment of stockpiles in disaster-
      prone areas.(5)

In fact, the disaster relief activities of UNDRO in the past few
years have considerably expanded beyond merely coordinating
the United Nations system's involvement, and the basic procedures adopted by the office for mobilization and coordination
have become increasingly effective.   Between March 1972 and
March 1977, UNDRO was involved in channeling almost $28
million for disaster relief in 91 disasters in 57 different countries, an average of about $300,000 per disaster.(6)
         UNDRO's Coordination Center in Geneva provides a
facility for rapid communication with over 90 potential disaster
relief donors, the League of Red Cross Societies (LORCS), and
with any telex subscriber anywhere in the world.   Information
disseminated goes not only to donors but also to many other
governments and agencies with a "need to know."   No government has committed funds to UNDRO in advance, so UNDRO
has no immediate capability to bring relief supplies to the
stricken area, apart from that conferred by the regular budget
provision for immediate response to disaster needs.   The
United States Agency for International Development has arranged to have all of its disaster-related messages to and from
its missions in a stricken country relayed automatically to
UNDRO.   As UNDRO's reputation has grown, more governments and other organizations outside, the United Nations
system have followed the United States lead and have also
increasingly relied upon UNDRO for advice and information.
         The United Nations Children's Fund (UNICEF), the Food
and Agriculture Organization (FAO), the World Food Programme (WFP) of FAO and the World Health Organization (WHO)
are other United Nations bodies which are nearly always active
in disaster relief operations.   UNICEF's primary responsibility
in disaster relief is the care of mothers and children, the most
vulnerable group of the population.   UNICEF has its own

system for the purchase and handling of supplies in Copenhagen and generates substantial funds through appeals to the general public for disaster relief operations. The Food and Agriculture Organization is responsible for relief and short-term recovery measures in the agricultural sector. The role of WFP is extremely important as it is the only United Nations agency specifically involved with emergency food assistance. The World Health organization purchases and ships medical supplies and equipment to disaster-affected areas. In some instances, WHO field teams may assist directly with relief operations. Most of these organizations have memoranda of understanding with UNDRO, specifying their operational responsibilities in relief activities and UNDRO's responsibility to coordinate disaster assistance and mobilize financial contribution.

When the government of a disaster-stricken country makes a request for relief assistance from UNDRO (which may be done through the office of the UNDP Resident Representative), this request is regarded as an appeal to the United Nations system in general. If requests for relief assistance are made directly to UNICEF, WHO, or FAO, UNDRO is consulted and advised of the action taken. UNDRO also informs the agencies involved in the relief situation of any contributions made to it, or known to have been made bilaterally to the disaster-stricken state by governmental and nongovernmental donors, that would modify or satisfy the request made to the agency or agencies concerned.

The UNDP Resident Representative is responsible for drawing together as a team the personnel of other Untied Nations agencies to work with representatives of potential donor governments, international voluntary agencies, and the Red Cross. This disaster team should exist before a disaster strikes, but, in many instances, it has not been so organized. This disaster team is activated when required, and when it has been activated it works in close association with the official government disaster relief authority. In some cases, the UNDP Resident Representative has served as the local coordinator of all external relief assistance at the request of the host government. In other cases, UNDRO sends experts to the disaster-affected country to assist the UNDP Resident Representative and the government in assessment and local coordination.

Since 1972, various special disaster relief units have been established within UNICEF, FAO, WFP, and WHO headquarters to coordinate the assistance directed by each organization with UNDRO and other relief donors. In addition to these recent administrative reforms, there have also been some attempts to codify the precise responsibilities of each organization in disaster relief. Most of these efforts have focused upon the respective responsibilities in relief activities with only very general reference to disaster prevention and preparedness. A notable exception in this regard is WHO - in particular, its Regional Office for the Americas, the Pan American Health Organization (PAHO), which recently formed its own emergency preparedness and disaster relief coordination unit. Clearly the emphasis on focusing the disaster relief efforts of the United Nations system in central offices and coordinating emergency assistance activities has been a priority within the past few years.

THE ROLE OF VOLUNTARY AGENCIES

Voluntary agencies, because of their historic tendency to work more closely with "grass roots" structures and because of their greater organizational flexibility, make substantial contributions to international disaster relief efforts. There are hundreds of voluntary agencies involved in international disaster relief. One study found over 70 voluntary agencies involved in a single disaster relief operation.(7) Some are strictly nongovernmental private organizations, while others may be more closely affiliated with governmental programs. Voluntary agencies play two major roles in the international relief system: 1) alerting the public and providing a channel for personal response to concern generated by the media; and 2) filling gaps in long-term development programs or providing alternative relief distribution systems (e.g., the Catholic groups in Latin America).

A number of widespead misconceptions have grown up about the private approach to disaster relief. Chief among them is the notion that voluntary agencies are "small-fry" operators in the international assistance game. In fact, there are many important roles that must be filled in any relief operation, and these are not limited to massive food and material assistance. Voluntary agencies are more likely to supplement the relief activities of other donors in relatively small amounts than to engage in highly visible, massive relief campaigns. Very often, their chief contribution is in the form of trained manpower to assist the relief efforts of the disaster-affected government. Because of this approach to disaster relief, there is a tendency to assume that their total contribution is minimal in relation to that of governmental organizations. Clearly, there is substantial evidence to dispute that point of view. For example, in the Sahelian drought relief operation, over $25 million was spent by voluntary agencies.(8) Collectively, voluntary agency contributions to disaster relief are substantial.

Another misconception about the private approach to disaster relief is that voluntary agencies are more politically independent and flexible than bilateral and multilateral governmental programs. Sometimes voluntary agencies have a greater number of organizational alternatives than the United Nations or bilateral donors, but they cannot act without heed to local political constraints. The view of the nongovernmental agency as a "nonpolitical," and therefore "neutral," actor (a characteristic also attributed to the United Nations) is sometimes perpetuated by various headquarters in their publicity, but it is not always borne out in practice.(9) Governments in disaster-stricken areas usually fail to perceive any real differences between external assistance, whether provided by private or public sources.

It is impossible to mention the accomplishments and operating procedures of all of the voluntary agencies that play a role in disaster relief. However, the International Red Cross system because of its size and universality, is a good place to start. Assistance to the victims of conflicts and natural disasters has been one of the primary functions of the Red Cross since its founding in 1861. Today, the Red Cross is the principal nongovernmental network for mobilizing and distributing international assistance in times of disaster, both natural and man-made.

David Holdsworth has best summed up the current status of the International Red Cross within the international disaster relief system.

> It possesses a name and a symbol which are universally recognized and often considered synonymous with dispassionate humanitarian assistance. It has been accorded a special status by governments and intergovernmental bodies, and has repeatedly served as the channel of assistance from other agencies in situations where it alone could act quickly or with the confidence of all parties. Its image is now so deeply ingrained in many parts of the world, particularly the Western world, that action by the Red Cross at the first stage of disasters is simply assumed by the public at large. In short, despite the relatively small scale of the assistance, the Red Cross is considered to be an important actor in the international relief system.(10)

The Red Cross movement has three basic organizational elements: 1) The International Committee of the Red Cross (ICRC), which is an independent, Geneva-based body composed of Swiss citizens, is concerned mainly with victims of armed conflict, 2) The National Societies, which are found at present in 125 countries, share the general principles and values of the Red Cross and conduct programs and activities directed toward the particular needs of their own countries. While many of these societies were initially founded to assist the war-wounded, their present activities, for the most part, revolve around disaster relief, health, and welfare. In some Moslem countries the national society operates as the Red Crescent Society, and, in Iran, as the Red Lion and Sun Society, 3) The League of Red Cross Societies (LORCS), which is the federation of the 125 national societies with a Secretariat in Geneva, was created after World War I. The League acts as the international spokesman of the national societies, assists the societies in their development, and coordinates international disaster relief.

One of the roles of the League during disaster relief operations is to maintain an information flow with donor societies. LORCS disaster circulars are also sent to all voluntary agencies which are members of the International Council of Voluntary Agencies (ICVA) Emergency Relief Committee, all diplomatic missions in Geneva, concerned United Nations agencies, and any other group which requests them.

Regular monthly meetings are held at the LORCS Secretariat in order to exchange information on current disaster situations. The meetings are attended by almost all international relief agencies, both governmental and nongovernmental, which are based in Geneva. The meetings are informal in nature, and the agencies aim to share information received from a disaster area and inform each other of their involvement in relief operations.

The LORCS-Volag Steering Committee was established in 1972 and is comprised of the League, Catholic Relief Service, Lutheran World Federation, OXFAM, and the World Council of Churches. Its main purpose is to provide a forum for exchange of experience and techniques in disaster preparedness and management and, especially, to share information on disaster situations; it also coordinates the response from appeals. The committee has undertaken several joint disaster-related studies, namely, the preparation of Country Fact Sheets, a National Disaster Preparedness Guide, and a Common Operational Handbook. The Country Fact Sheets are presently being reviewed, especially their medical and nutritional part. This study is being done in cooperation with WHO and PAHO and is being undertaken by the Center for Research on Disaster Epidemiology in Brussels.

LORCS has a formal monitoring system for disaster relief operations. It sends delegates to work with the various national societies and to assist them in carrying out relief operations. These delegates report to Geneva on the progress of the operation and the national societies are required to accept LORCS' participation in monitoring disaster relief activities.

Most voluntary agencies, unlike LORCS, are primarily

involved in development programs, and disaster relief is only one segment of their total spectrum of activities. Voluntary agencies, like governments and the United Nations agencies, suffer from a "time/money lag" problem in their approach to disaster relief operations. This stems from the way in which they raise money for relief. The emergency situation may proceed to the longer-term rehabilitation and development phase before substantial resources to mobilize relief operations can be obtained. This problem creates a tendency to blur the distinction between relief and development approaches.

Other major problems affecting voluntary agencies derive from the difficulties in coordinating their activities with other elements in the international disaster relief system. While a rather effective arrangement between LORCS and UNDRO has been established, smaller private agencies which do not co-ordinate with any of the established coordinating bodies still create some problems. The liaison links between voluntary agency headquarters and their field offices are variable, and the information flow between agencies and governmental donors is many times not as good as it should be. Better liaison needs to be established in-country with the disaster-stricken government and other relief donors. Thus the coordination issue, one of the primary problems in the international disaster relief system for all elements involved, is particularly crucial for voluntary agencies.

THE ROLE OF THE MEDIA

Often the first news of a major natural disaster event comes from the international media. Large-scale damage and loss of life is always a newsworthy event and the attendant publicity moves the international community to respond generously with offers of assistance to the disaster-stricken area.

Disaster victims and the well-meaning donor community are indebted to the international media. Many times corruption of government officials, badly administered relief operations, gaps between the real needs of victims and the needs per-ceived by a government or relief donors have been brought to the world's attention by the international media. The media often support and assist in the dissemination of rumors and substantiate reports of outbreaks of communicable diseases following major disasters. The international media also provide very useful publicity for all the achievements made by relief donors and assist in the fund-raising campaigns for a disaster assistance operation. All of these benefits of media disaster coverage and the accompanying relief operations cannot be discounted, and the importance of the media in shaping our

ideas about what is happening in a remote part of the world
cannot be overemphasized.

Despite these notable contributions, the media can be a
source of problems during and after a disaster relief operation.
One reporter has offered this view of the role of the international media in disasters: "Sometimes there is no greater
disaster than the Western press!"(11)   The cause of these
disparaging words may stem from two general kinds of problems the media may inadvertently create.   The first concerns
the relationship between the media and the government of a
disaster-stricken area, specifically the demands made upon an
already overworked bureaucracy, and the second results from
government attempts to suppress or control information about
the disaster and the relief operations.

The first problem arises from the fact that there are
many different kinds of reporters and all have different needs
when they arrive in a disaster-stricken area.   Some use a wire
service and may demand typewriters and telephones; some use
the television medium and need facilities to accommodate their
camera equipment.   Many newsmen are low-paid, but some are
"star" reporters who may demand filet mignon and an interview
with the king.   Most reporters fall somewhere in between these
extremes, but all have communication needs and must have a
way of getting their information or film out of the disaster
zone.   Many reporters demand an eyewitness tour of the area
affected and, therefore, require transport and accommodations
(food, lodging).   Government officials may have to make very
unpleasant choices in the face of competing demands by
reporters.   Decisions may have to be made about whether to
commit a helicopter, which is badly needed to airlift relief
commodities, to transport reporters to the disaster site.
Government officials realize all too well the value in eliciting
sympathetic reporting of their situation.   Good public relations
with the international media mean more support for the relief
operation.

Government's censorship and control of the reporting of a
disaster relief operation may complicate the situation to the
point where reporting becomes difficult.   Governmental refusal
to respond to reporters' inquiries is attributable to more than
one factor - inefficiency, inability to confirm rumors, national
security concern, and occasionally attempts to cover-up a
deteriorating or dishonest situation.   However, when efforts
are made to suppress information during a disaster situation,
reporters accustomed to more freedom may become suspicious of
government corruption, scandal, and black marketing and may
deliberately look for an exposé story to write.   These problems
can be circumvented if governments report any misconduct
they find to press before the press discovers it.   In this way,
reporters may be prevented from getting the impression that
the government is part of a conspiracy against the disaster
victims.

Most often government censorship is not a deliberate policy, although there are exceptions. Rather, the situation is usually very complex, and/or governments refuse or may not be able to aid reporters. An honest exchange of information and a sincere effort on both sides to deal with the situation realistically and openly can only benefit the disaster victims and may serve to improve relationships and, therefore, the functioning of the international disaster relief system.

PROBLEM AREAS IN INTERNATIONAL DISASTER RELIEF OPERATIONS

There are a number of issues that arise in connection with international disaster relief coordination. These issues can be grouped into two general categories: 1) the specification and diversification of relief activities by numerous donors, that is, operational coordination; and 2) the relationships between different relief donors and between donors and recipients regarding jurisdiction and authority, that is, policy coordination.

Operations Coordination

One of the most difficult problems of disaster relief coordination occurs with the voluntary agencies. Voluntary agencies are far from a homogeneous group. They have major philosophical and religious differences, differences in expertise and geographical involvement, and vast differences in the size of their operations and their budgets. While their differences sometimes make it difficult to work together, their similarities also create problems for relief coordination.

Competition for funding and recognition is a major coordination problem. Many voluntary agencies appeal for public funds from the same general constituency, and this results in a money-raising competitiveness that is seldom conducive to relief coordination. A notable effort to alleviate this problem has been made by the United Kingdom's Disasters Emergency Committee, composed of five major British voluntary agencies (OXFAM, War on Want, Save the Children, Christian Aid, and the British National Red Cross), which jointly appeal after a disaster and jointly agree on the use of the proceeds of the appeal.

A study of the Sahelian relief operation cites the "pressure to spend" phenomenon which affects coordination of both public and private activities.(12) Voluntary agencies are primarily funded by private contributions. When the general public becomes aware of a disaster, it wants to know what its favorite charity is doing to help. Thus, voluntary agencies must be responsive to their constituencies. This pressure from the public to "be seen doing something" is transferred from headquarters to the field offices. In some cases, by the time funds are raised the crisis is over, and field offices are faced with too much money too late and too few new projects on which to spend the funds. In order to assist fund raising and justify expenditures made, a type of publicity which has become known as "starving-baby advertising" is often used to arouse the sympathies of the donating public.

At the field level voluntary agency coordination is sometimes better, particularly if there is a permanent field contingent. There are many cases of local coordinating groups being established, but the time and effort spent on coordinating and information sharing is necessarily limited. Even the large voluntary agencies usually have only very small field offices.

This description of some of the basic problems facing voluntary agency coordination does not mean to suggest that all is well with regard to governments and the United Nations. The major problems of relief operations involve coordination between the different elements of the United Nations disaster relief system. Since 1972, the structure of this system has changed considerably, and relief donors now operate with more information about what other types of assistance are being given to disaster victims. Some difficult problems still remain, however.

Resolution 2816 (XXVI), which established the Office of the United Nations Disaster Relief Coordinator (UNDRO), was intended to strengthen and make more effective the collective efforts of the international community, particularly the United Nations system, in the field of disaster assistance. The mandate given the Disaster Relief Coordinator was extremely wide - too wide to be fulfilled with the staff then provided. Although more posts have since been added, half of them are still financed from voluntary contributions to a trust fund which has only a limited life. This has been a complicating and delaying factor in recruiting staff for all the authorized posts. Despite these limitations, UNDRO has made considerable progress in the field of disaster relief coordination.

It is almost unknown for UNDRO to get the <u>first</u> news of a disaster from the UNDP Resident Representative. There are many other sources of information - governments, voluntary agencies, the media - which may bring a particularly hazardous situation to the Coordinator's attention. Disasters such as hurricanes, typhoons, and earthquakes are usually public knowledge soon after they occur. Therefore, the problem of detection, except in remote areas or in cases of slowly developing or "creeping" disasters, is not a serious one. Once a disaster has been detected, however, the process of bringing relief to the victims begins.

The United Nations system of organizations, including UNDRO, cannot initiate any relief activity without a request from the government concerned. Fig. 2.1, which is a far too simplified view of disaster relief communicating within the United Nations, does serve to illustrate somewhat the channels through which messages are often transmitted.

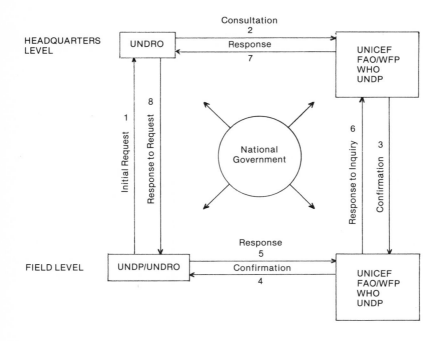

Fig. 2.1. Headquarters – Field Coordination in the United Nations Disaster Relief System

Initial requests from governments may be submitted to the UNDP field office, and then are relayed to UNDRO (no. 1). However, requests may originate spontaneously from a country or may result from discussions with the country after disclosure of a disaster. A government's request may also reach United Nations agencies' headquarters directly or through the local or regional representative. When requests reach UNDRO, that Office may consult with specialized agencies' headquarters to verify the information received (no. 2). Confirmation of initial relief requests and damage surveys involves exchanges with each agency's field representative, the respective headquarters (no. 3), and UNDP in the field (no. 4). Response from the UNDP field office (no. 5) is evaluated, and the appropriate agency representative is consulted. This opinion is then relayed to headquarters (no. 6), reevaluated, and submitted to UNDRO (no. 7). UNDRO coordinates each agency's response with other relief donors and informs the disaster-stricken government through the UNDP field office (no. 8). The UNDP Resident Representative coordinates relief activities at the field level.

The United Nations disaster relief system is characterized by two types of focal points - one at headquarters and one in the field. The purpose of a focal point is not just to coordinate information but also to direct resources to the disaster-stricken area. The communications at the field level could be improved considerably between the UNDP and other specialized agency field representatives. Regionalization within the organization may complicate the communications between field and headquarters disaster relief focal points. For example, WHO headquarters confirmation would be requested from the regional office, which, in turn, would request confirmation and information from the country representative. Response to the inquiry (no. 6) would transmit from the field through the regional office to WHO in Geneva.

Policy Coordination

Because there are several organizations involved in the United Nations disaster relief system, it is natural that some questions would arise regarding UNDRO's responsibilities. One of these issues concerns the type of disaster with which UNDRO is to be involved. A comprehensive report by the Secretary-General identified sudden and unpredictable disasters as falling within the mandate, but,

> For scarcity and famine...are rarely sudden and unpredictable and to this extent fall largely outside the arrangements proposed....(13)

This is because the arrangements proposed that the Co-ordinator would be competent to deal with natural disasters which are on a scale and of a kind that require relief assistance from several different sources (including more than one organization of the United Nations system), and which therefore require coordination efforts. The Secretary-General's report pointed out that in emergencies which develop in a gradual way like droughts and crop failures, FAO and WFP would normally be able to deal with the situation, and UNDRO's coordination efforts would not be needed. An example of this limitation occurred in 1973, when FAO was appointed coordinator for the international relief operation in the Sahelian zone of West Africa. However, later that year UNDRO became involved in the relief operations in Ethiopia as a result of drought and famine.

A second question arises concerning the relationship of UNDRO to other United Nations organizations involved in man-made disaster relief situations. Apart from natural disasters, Resolution 2816 (XXVI) also covers "other disaster situations." According to a United Nations Legal Counsel opinion, this expression would ordinarily cover man-made disasters.(14) However, the Secretary-General's report excluded any kind of man-made disaster, although it recognized that:

> The effects of civil conflicts or emergencies caused
> by war or civil disturbances have many of the
> features associated with natural disasters.(15)

Furthermore, when the preparatory work of the resolution is examined, it reveals that there was, in fact, no agreement among the cosponsors about it.(16) If UNDRO's mandate were to include man-made disasters, this interpretation would raise jurisdictional conflicts with the Office of the United Nations High Commissioner for Refugees and could even enable the Coordinator to intervene in internal conflicts which fall within the competence of member states.

Policy coordination difficulties can also arise as a result of political problems within a disaster-stricken country. In other words, governments are often subject to many complex political prssures that arise during a disaster relief operation and complicate the process of getting humanitarian assistance to those in need. For example, the effect of a population discovering that its government was mismanaging or not coping with a developing disaster situation or relief situation has meant political death for several government regimes. There are many influences and forces at work both within and outside a disaster-affected area that would welcome information about a disaster situation, particularly if the marketing or producing countries concerned had surpluses which could be directed there for profit. Furthermore, disasters hurt the tourist industry; there have been many cases of government denials of a disaster situation because the livelihood of the country was so dependent upon tourism.

Many governments feel that asking for relief is paramount to admitting imcompetence or mismanagement. Therefore, even in the face of almost certain disaster, there is some hesitancy to acknowledge publicly such a situation. This is commonly known as the acknowledgment problem. It has affected the ability of the international disaster relief system to perform effectively in several instances in recent years.

There has always been a tension in the international community between the claims of national sovereignty, as evidenced by the doctrine of nonintervention and the claims by the international community for human rights, which argue for interference to assist individuals for humanitarian reasons. This argument has gained particular momentum in the past few years due to the increasing involvement of governments and multilateral and private organizations in relief to victims of man-made disasters like the civil wars in Indonesia, Nigeria and Pakistan, as well as natural disasters in Ethiopia and the Sahel. Experience in these situations seems to indicate that some action should be taken to clarify the responsibilities of disaster-affected governments and international donors in providing assistance to victims of natural disasters.

A survey of the political problems associated with disasters indicates that political problems are a regular, rather than a random or extraordinary, feature of natural disasters. The most commonly reported problem concerns acknowledgment of the disaster by the government of the stricken country, followed by political decisions by donors, government interference with the relief or rehabilitation process for political reasons, and corruption of the distribution of relief. Political problems are reported in one of every three disasters, with drought being the most prone to political problems.(17)

Another problem which plagues the policy maker has to do with resource scarcity and the overriding commitment to development objectives. Disaster has not infrequently been referred to as "Band-aid therapy" and therefore a waste of resources in terms of attacking the real problems of poverty in the developing world. This attitude no doubt arises from the quite justifiable recognition that the impact of disaster in the future can only be lessened by long-term development efforts.

A reliance on relief as the only strategy for surmounting the problems of disaster is a waste, but some form of international assistance to the victims of disasters will always be needed despite large-scale development investments. The question is not really whether or not to invest in disaster relief, but rather to make an appropriate technical assessment and spend the money wisely. The issue is how to avoid unnecessary expenses and ineffective measures during disaster relief. It is a problem of quality rather than quantity.

SUMMARY

In terms of cost-benefit or priorities analyses, it may be too costly to rectify the real problems of the international disaster relief system. On the other hand, ways of alleviating some of the relief-related problems are known or have been recommended. Yet for one reason or another - political expediency, lack of resources, lack of concern - the will of governments and organizations to pursue these recommendations and make changes in the international disaster relief system surfaces only intermittently. The interest in reform is strong when a crisis is new, but it fades when the crisis continues or when several months pass without a really major disaster. The attention span with regard to disaster relief reform is also very short when it becomes clear that solutions required to deal effectively with the problem may be difficult to implement and will involve sacrifice on the part of the recipient and the donor.

The international disaster relief system has great potential to respond quickly and appropriately to relieve human suffering caused by natural disasters. However, there are some deeply rooted coordination problems which impede the efficient performance of this system. Programs which promote disaster preparedness planning in disaster-prone developing countries could alleviate some of the coordination problems which arise in disaster relief situations.

The major donors of international disaster relief have a very direct and immediate interest in promoting the establishment or upgrading of national disaster relief organizations and national disaster plans in poor and disaster-prone countries. Hundreds of millions of dollars are given annually to disaster-affected countries, often on the basis of inaccurate information about the disaster or the needs of the victims, and often with little or no assurance that the assistance given will reach the intended recipients. National disaster preparedness planning could alleviate some of the worst of these difficulties and greatly contribute to easing complex logistical and coordination problems attendant to every disaster relief situation.

The problems of disaster relief coordination within and between governments, international organizations, and voluntary agencies cannot be resolved overnight. With proper planning and foresight and a realization that coordination saves lives, many of these difficulties can be worked out in advance and the victims of disasters will no longer be the victims of unplanned international relief efforts as well.

3 Disaster Preparedness

Disaster prevention and preparedness form a system of enormous scope which involves official and voluntary organizations at national, regional, and local levels, the general public directly in a number of critical aspects, and activities in almost any time scale from a few minutes to several decades.(1) In general, prevention covers long-term aspects and is concerned with policies and programs to prevent or eliminate the occurrence of disasters. Preparedness covers the short-term aspects and is designed to include the action necessary during the approach of a possible disaster, during the existence of a disaster situation, and in the ensuing period devoted to relief and rehabilitation.

Disaster prevention depends on the application of science and technology to prevent disasters. Two types of preventive strategy are usually employed - one which relates to problems of land use, zoning, building construction, and the planning of human settlements, and the other which involves the prediction, warning and control of natural phenomena which often result in disaster.(2) Policies for disaster prevention should be closely allied to economic, social and environmental policies, so that the cost-benefit elements of disaster prevention may be clearly incorporated into the national planning process.

Because disasters are formidable obstacles to development, disaster prevention measures not only save lives and diminish physical damage, but they also help to safeguard the economic development of the country concerned. Despite the potential of disaster prevention programs, in many disaster-prone countries, very little is now being done to prevent or mitigate the effects of the next major disaster. There are several reasons why these countries have not placed a high priority on disaster prevention.

Foremost are financial considerations. While it is well

32

recognized that disasters have the greatest economic and social impact in the poorest of the developing countries, these countries often cannot afford to divert development resources to large-scale, long-term, and often costly, prevention schemes. For example, rebuilding and relocating a city like Managua, Nicaragua would involve an inestimable cost and many years to complete. The social and political disruption of such a scheme would probably be an insurmountable obstacle to this and many other large-scale disaster-prone regions which should not be inhabited. For example, alluvial flood plains are very attractive for habitation because they are agriculturally rich and have great importance to economic growth, but they are also very hazardous locations for human habitation.

While economic cost-benefit arguments are often used to explain the reluctance of developing countries to institute greater measures of disaster prevention, in many regions, particularly in the developing areas, these arguments are most difficult to apply because of the many intangible benefits and social constraints involved. Local tradition and experience are probably sufficient justification, in many cases, to indicate that all costs outweigh all benefits, economic and otherwise.

Disaster prevention is as much a question of risk mitigation as it is of total risk elimination, simply because the latter is not always possible. Disaster mitigation may involve land-use reforms, revision and enforcement of zoning regulations, revised building codes, application of engineering designs to reduce hazards, etc. Sometimes the most effective mitigation measures are the most inexpensive. In order to be effective, however, long-term strategies for the prevention and mitigation of disasters must be seen as an integral part of any development program. Many competing concerns within a country complicate the development process, and it may be politically unwise for a government to invest in an unpopular prevention scheme when faced with other priorities.

A further problem is a psychological one, involving a society's attitude toward disasters. Many societies experience a sense of fatalism about natural disasters. This may be due to cultural or religious beliefs, or may arise because of the enormity of the problem, successive disasters, and the lack of resources to plan for assistance in emergency situations. Related to this problem, is the belief that the people's traditional ways of preventing hazardous conditions from developing will continue to serve adequately, and that it is too great a task to reeducate a population which has used these methods for generations. Despite the great potential benefits of long-term disaster prevention strategies, the poorest countries need an interim measure.

NATURE AND SCOPE OF THE CONCEPT

An interim measure which can be taken, and a strategy of action which should accompany disaster prevention measures, is a program of disaster preparedness. A program of preparedness for dealing with disasters once they occur, rather than for preventing them, is a less financially demanding course of action in terms of planning, resources and time. Many aspects of disaster preparedness require relatively few economic resources, and are more a product of awareness and understanding than expensive long-term commitments.

Preparedness means a readiness to cope with disaster situations which cannot be avoided. This involves warning the affected population, developing an operational plan of action and an organization to manage and coordinate that action, the training of personnel in rescue and relief techniques, the stockpiling of supplies and the earmarking of funds for relief operations. While advocates of disaster preparedness do not deny the logic of disaster prevention, or the returns that in theory are possible, they are sceptical about the likelihood of achieving them in practice. Although preparedness and prevention complement one another and ideally should be pursued simultaneously, lacking the resources and time to invest in prevention, preparedness seems like a reasonable interim measure for the poorest of the disaster-prone developing countries.

The state of disaster preparedness in a country is a measure of the capability of the country and its people to take the various steps needed to safeguard lives and property during three successive phases: when disaster threatens, while the adverse conditions that could result in disaster actually exist, and during the recovery period that follows. When these conditions moderate or move away, a period of rehabilitation follows and, in some aspects at least, rehabilitation merges into a process, which may be a very lengthy one of reconstruction. These conditions illustrate the continuous and cyclical nature of the various components of disaster prevention and preparedness. A disaster brings one cycle to an end and initiates the next one. Figure 3.1 illustrates the cylical nature of disaster and the role of disaster preparedness within this cycle.

Too often countries with disaster-prone histories have done little to prepare in advance for natural disasters. In many countries no contingency plan has been prepared or relief organization established which could resolve the kinds of questions which inevitably arise in every disaster situation where international assistance is required. Who has the authority within the government to request assistance and coordinate the relief effort? Have responsibilities and oper-

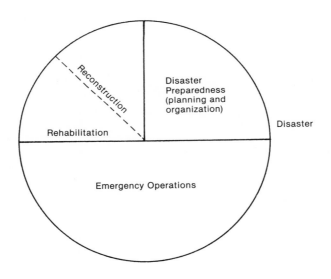

Fig. 3.1. The Disaster Cycle

Source: United States Agency for International Development,
"International Disaster Preparedness Seminar Instruction Guidelines," Washington, D.C.: U.S. Department of State, 1976, p.
iv.

ational roles been assigned at the federal and local levels?
What resources are available within the country that can be
immediately released for use in a disaster and where are they
located?   Who is responsible for damage assessment and estimates of relief requirements?   Who is responsible for in-
country communications and liaison with foreign governmental
and nongovernmental donors, as well as with international
organizations?

The poorest of the disaster-prone developing countries are quite often characterized by a lack of managerial skill, which makes the development of an efficient emergency preparedness plan unlikely without international assistance. The critical importance of administrative planning has been pointed out by one writer who states:

> Although the natural phenomena cause havoc, death and destruction, the resultant distress affecting the survivors is, at least in part, caused by the Administration's difficulty in maintaining the life support systems. Confusion and delay in getting assistance to those in need have resulted in countless unnecessary deaths.(3)

Administrative support for the disaster-stricken government, until recently, has not been a feature of most foreign and international organization disaster assistance programs. Since the main responsibility for direction and coordination of a disaster relief operation lies with the disaster-stricken government, there is usually a tremendeous strain on the administrative capabilities of the bureaucracy.

The institution of disaster preparedness programs not only offers opportunities to improve disaster relief operations, but also offers a wide range of potential benefits for economic and social development. The following discussion indicates some of the areas of concern in pre-disaster planning.

Prediction and Warning

In the past few years substantial progress has been made to improve man's ability to detect potential disaster conditions and to warn the affected population to take emergency precautionary measures. The value of past investment in prediction and warning capabilities is clearly demonstrable. Despite the increasing property losses, there has been a notable decline in lives lost when such capabilities have been established.

Atmospheric phenomena can be predicted with greater accuracy than earth disturbances. While the potential for earthquakes, volcanoes, and landslides may be known, precise prediction and warning of the timing and extent of destruction is not currently feasible. However, certain types of disasters such as river floods, droughts and forest fires are presaged by discernible weather factors and changes and can be predicted. In many cases, the existing prediction and warning capabilities are quite sound and accurate.

The tropical cyclone in the Bay of Bengal, which brought such tragic consequences to Bangladesh in November 1970, became a starting point for focusing international attention upon the need for cyclone warning systems. Around this time, a series - of typhoons also struck the Philippines, causing heavy loss of life and damage. The Intergovernmental Typhoon Committee, established in 1968 by the Economic and Social Commission for Asia and the Pacific (ESCAP) and the World Meteorological Organization (WMO), appealed to the United Nations for international action. In response to this appeal, a General Assembly resolution called upon WMO, with the help of other organizations and member states of the United Nations, to mobilize scientists and resources to discover ways of mitigating the harmful effects of these storms and of removing or minimizing their destructive potential.(4) WMO accordingly set up a Tropical Cyclone Project, which is the framework for a plan of action covering the detection and forecasting of tropical cyclones, the forecasting of floods and storm surges, the organization of early warning systems, and certain other aspects of disaster prevention and preparedness. The activities of the ESCAP/WMO Typhoon Committee have evoked growing attention in other areas affected by tropical cyclones. A direct consequence has been the establishment of two other regional bodies, one for the countries around the Bay of Bengal and the Arabian Sea and the other for countries in the southwest Indian Ocean.

However, there remains a very fundamental problem with early warning systems, once the potential disaster hazard has been detected. This involves the dissemination of the warning message. Many lives have been lost because a warning system was unable to carry out its responsibilities satisfactorily. An early warning system is useless without a way to relay the information in an understandable way to the population in danger. An example of this type of problem occurred on November 19, 1977, when a cyclone from the Bay of Bengal struck the state of Andhra Pradesh on the east coast of India, leaving over 10,000 people dead and thousands homeless. Just a week earlier, the nearby state of Tamil Nadu had been struck by a cyclone of nearly equal intensity and only 500 people lost their lives. Disaster preparedness made the difference in the two incidents. The meteorology department did warn the government of a cyclone four days before the Andhra Pradesh tragedy, but the people were not prepared enough for the ordeal. In some areas, the warnings did not reach the people in the scattered, vulnerable villages for want of effective communication facilities and warning systems. It was reported from interviews with residents of the areas that,

> ...crying wolf too often over the years has seriously reduced the credibility of the warnings. The task before the weathermen is to win greater credibility by improving the accuracy of their forecasts over a reasonably long period.(5)

The experience of countries where disaster preparedness
is well developed and is constantly being improved confirms
that an effective warning system makes a major contribution to
the safety of human lives. A feature of the warning system,
as of the short-term measures which result in disaster preparedness, is that the action which follows the issue of a
warning must involve the general public, as well as those who
have specific responsibilities in the relief operation.

Disaster Legislation

An adequate disaster law describes the responsibilities of
a government in the case of a disaster, establishes a disaster
relief organization, provides for preparedness and relief
measures, and specifically authorizes the organization to perform its tasks with full cooperation of all concerned.

A comprehensive system of legislation related to disasters
contains two basic types of laws: one category concerned with
long-term construction and reconstruction with the purposes of
disaster prevention or mitigation, and the other concerned with
preparedness for an actual emergency or short-term recovery.
These two classes of legislation are not entirely separate and
independent, but are linked by overlapping features, just as
preparedness and prevention have overlapping features.

Legislation is necessary to provide the authority and
assure cooperation and assistance among often competing government jurisdictions. The concentration of decision-making
powers and financial resources in the central government may
not be conducive to rapid intervention on the scene of a disaster. On the other hand, it may not be possible to use the
regional or local government institutions and resources without
the authorization of the central agencies and the allocation of
special credits. In the absence of precise instructions, local
authorities may consider that it is not their responsibility to
take the initiative. This attitude is sometimes carried to the
point of complete indifference to the situation in general. The
dispersion of similar or overlapping powers among different
ministries and departments leads to duplication or gaps, which
inevitably impede the effective organization of relief.

There are sometimes difficulties in realizing this aspect of
disaster preparedness in developing countries. Some of the
difficulties can be attributed to a desire to keep ultimate
authority with the central government figure. This may be
desirable given the highly politicized nature of a disaster
situation. For example, disasters often have provided enough
disruption to result in the overthrow of political regimes
(Ethiopia, Niger). However, it is precisely this issue that
supports the case for the legal establishment of a disaster
relief authority. Much of the confusion attending disaster

relief operations could be alleviated in advance if authority and responsibility were firmly established by law. Because the disaster relief authority must coordinate and utilize skills, personnel and resources from other governments, international organizations, private and voluntary agencies, it is necessary to authorize these relationships in the laws, decrees and regulations. Lines of responsibility must specifically describe the legal status of the disaster relief authority to enable action.

Disaster Organization

Most countries which have instituted disaster preparedness procedures have found it useful to establish a central coordinating force to direct the human and material resources of the country for disaster relief. Two basic principles seem to emerge: First, disaster planning and management must follow the normal administrative structure with the same channels of communication, responsibility and authority delegated within the same departments of expertise. It is important that a government's emergency response to natural disasters be accomplished through existing organizational arrangements, augmented as necessary. Emergency operations should only be a logical extension of the government's dealings with day-to-day emergencies. This ensures a greater acceptance by the disaster victims of the services provided and cooperation with the rescue and relief personnel. This is an obvious and important implication, especially in the health sector.

Secondly, the ultimate responsibility for both planning and coordinating disaster preparedness and relief operations must rest with one individual through a centralized administration. Ideally, the national disaster relief coordinator should be a permanent full-time position. The "two-hat" system, in which personnel assume disaster relief coordination duties in addition to their regular duties, has led, in many instances, to the neglect of preparedness under the pressure of other activities. Just as disaster preparedness has remained an afterthought within development programs, the preparedness duties of a national disaster relief coordinator have suffered because of the "two-hat" system. However, one must take a practical approach. The availability of trained men and women in developing countries makes it improbable that the disaster coordinator will assume only this position of responsibility. Using personnel on a temporary basis to prepare for and perform disaster relief assignments ensures the availability of capable staff from within the existing government agencies and the cooperative coordination of private and voluntary agencies.

There are a number of activities beyond the direction and coordination of relief operations with which a disaster organization should be concerned. The national disaster relief organization should maintain liaison with national and international offices of a technical and scientific character. Hazard analysis and prevention studies should be gathered, technical information from meteorological and hydrological agencies obtained, and evaluation procedures for disaster relief operations established. One idea of how such an organization might be structured is shown in Fig. 3.2.

Although centralized coordination is important at the national level, it is also important to have corresponding authority delegated at the local levels. The local level (e.g., district, village) is the most important relief organization level because it is the closest to the people. It is at this level that the emergency is felt most keenly, and protection, rescue, and relief operations are launched and carried out. It is here that damage is assessed and requirements evaluated, so that the necessary action can be taken with the speed and efficiency required.

Disaster Plan

A disaster plan is an exercise in the anticipation of what might happen and what might be required in a relief situation. Its purpose includes taking steps to insure that the disaster response is organized and effective. Planning must include how the available human and material resources for relief will be integrated into an efficient and manageable operation. This must extend to the United Nations, foreign and international relief agencies of all kinds, and to local voluntary organizations.

Planning requires the cooperation of all levels of government. To be confident that disaster planning is preparing government officials and the public to cope better with disasters, such plans must be exercised and evaluated. A disaster relief organization without a plan is practically useless.

Each disaster is unique to the extent that no two disasters are very closely similar in their many and varied aspects. However, there are a number of features which are common to all disasters and help to guide the plan of action that must be taken.

When pre-disaster planning has been undertaken, it has been possible to inform donors (both within and outside the affected country) of relief requirements. External assistance is intended only to supplement a nation's own relief efforts; thus a knowledge of the internal resources is necessary in order to communicate accurate information to the international community. A key element, therefore, in a national disaster plan is a provision for assessing relief requirements, available

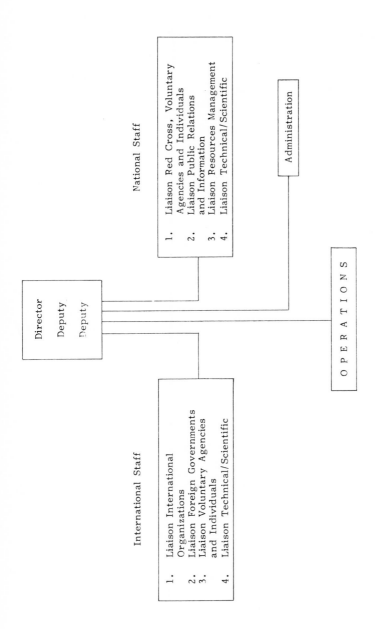

Fig. 3.2. Office of the National Disaster Relief Coordinator

Source: U.S. Agency for International Development, Office of Foreign Disaster Assistance, "International Disaster Preparedness; Instruction Guidelines, Washington, D.C.: U.S. Department of State p. 36.

in-country resources, and the net emergency assistance required from the international community.

Frequently, disaster situations require continuous round-
the-clock activity, and therefore, the establishment of an
emergency operations center which would serve as the actual
control for the relief operation. The control of information is
a critical element in any relief operation, and communications
with services such as medical, police, fire, and telecommuni-
cations is essential for a successful operation. From such a
center, operating on a continuous basis, coordination and
integration of services directed to the disaster area can be
controlled.

It is most important that a disaster plan be not just a
"paper plan," but a working guide to action. This requires
that the plan be exercised in order to discover its faults and
evaluated in order to make improvements in its provisions. A
disaster plan should not be prepared and then forgotten, but
should be continually updated and improved. A plan on paper
which has never been tried has very little chance of working
when it is needed.

Public Education

Public awareness of the threats posed by various natural
disasters is essential to preparing for them and reducing their
destructive effects. Public information and education should
be an essential component of disaster preparedness. If the
general public is kept fully and constantly informed of the
dangerous conditions which can cause disasters, the organization and operation of a disaster preparedness system has
every chance of working. In this context, education is the
natural complement to the provision of information. An
educational program, designed at an appropriate level for
children and adults, should give basic knowledge about the
nature of the risks involved and about warning services and
protective measures. Educational programs should be supplemented by campaigns through the press, radio and television. When media are lacking, posters and pictures in local
languages can be distributed. Concentrating disaster preparedness efforts at the local level is critical to the success of
any public information campaign.

Public education and the provision of information should
be designed to meet local requirements as closely as practica-
ble. Educating the public and providing information, however,
is not sufficient to ensure that people will respond to warnings. Warnings must be supplemented by clear instructions
telling the public what it should do. "The objective is to
create a partnership beteen government and people so that
disaster preparedness is recognized as a joint responsibility."(6)

An increasing number of developing countries are recognizing the need for educating the public in a systematic
way on the dangers of disasters and on the value of disaster
preparedness. This is particularly noticeable in countries
bordering the west Pacific where typhoons occur frequently
and cause enormous damage.

In Japan, education on disaster preparedness is com-
pulsory in schools and courses are given on safety measures
and on evacuation of danger areas. The first day of September each year is observed as "Disaster Prevention Day,"
and numerous activities are organized to remind the public of
the dangers of typhoons and the associated floods and storm
surges. In the Philippines, courses are offered in elementary
and secondary schools, in institutions for adult education, as
well as in colleges for the training of teachers, engineers etc.
In Australia, the inhabitants of areas which are vulnerable to
tropical cyclones are given intensive basic and refresher
courses on tropical cyclones, warning systems and actions to
be taken. Education continues to be of major importance in
countries like Japan, the Philippines and Australia, where the
organization of disaster prevention and preparedness has
reached a highly developed stage.

While public education has great potential, by itself it is
not sufficient as disaster preparedness strategy. What is
needed is nonformal education. Continuing education should
be undertaken so that individuals will not be permitted to
neglect the negative consequences of their activities. While
education can counteract the natural tendency to do the wrong
thing, the basis for this knowledge must be constantly re-
freshed and renewed. For example, in order to encourage
someone to fix the roof before the rains begin, one must
continually be reminded of what it was like when it was
raining.

Michal Lechat has underscored the need for continuing
education in another context when describing the lack of
awareness of a population to disasters.

> People in communities which were wiped out by a
> nearby volcano some eighty years ago were playing
> cards on a night when the volcano was again be-
> ginning to erupt. Subsequent explanations included
> the idea that it was only a flying saucer which had
> landed on the next island with a few Martians
> aboard.(7)

While public education should first be directed to the
people of a disaster-prone area, those in principal positions of
responsibility in the country also need programs of education.
Related to public education is the specialized training of government officials and disaster relief administrators.

Disaster Relief Training

There is a definite need for some kind of training for all professional workers in disaster-prone countries, be they agricultural extension agents, community workers or para-medical personnel. Investment of this sort would be more profitable in the long run than sending in expatriate rescue and relief teams.

Disaster relief coordinators should have the kind of training which would increase their awareness of disaster hazards in neighboring countries with similar problems. A regional approach to disaster management training is beneficial not only because of similar problems, cultures, and levels of economic development, but also because it fosters regional cooperation in solving disaster-related problems. Cooperation in the study of problems and in the development of ways to solve them regionally is also likely to make the provision of funds and specialists' advice from the United Nations, inter-national, and other sources more economical and easier to arrange.(8)

One of the responsibilities of the national and district disaster relief organizations should be to institute in-county training programs for other personnel involved in disaster relief operations. The disaster relief organization should ensure that the appropriate ministries have some provision for training in emergency procedures, or in soliciting and training a volunteer corps which could be activated in the event of a disaster. The staff of any disaster relief organization needs to be trained in the general responsibilities of its organization, and the particular procedures involved in ensuring cooperation at the ministerial and local levels, as well as with foreign donors.

It is not necessary to have a standing army of personnel trained in relief and rescue techniques. When disaster strikes, most rescues are made by neighbors or relatives immediately after the impact. Full use should be made of volunteers, police and fire departments, since many of them have the necessary training to form a relief corps which can be coordinated by the disaster relief organization.

Not too surprisingly, countries which are already reasonably well prepared want to do more, whereas those countries which almost totally lack any form of disaster pre-paredness are unable or unwilling to get started. Those countries with established programs of disaster preparedness should be used as models for the development of programs elsewhere.

In some countries, notably Australia, Japan and the United States, highly developed systems already exist for disaster prevention and preparedness. Where sustained efforts have been applied to prevention and preparedness, there is a strong awareness that the time never comes when everything possible has been done. The protective arrangements, whether long-term or short-term, are under constant scrutiny to find ways of improving them, and each disaster is followed by a review of the functioning of the disaster organization and plan and of the public response. Other countries which are conscious of what can be done and should be done in the area of disaster preparedness are making strenuous efforts to achieve greater development and higher standards of efficiency. In still other countries, protective measures that exist are mostly in the rudimentary stage. It is the second and third groups of countries - those which have made a good start in the development of disaster preparedness and those still in the very early stages of pre-disaster planning - which are the subject of the following discussion.

PREPAREDNESS IN DISASTER-PRONE COUNTRIES

The subject of disaster preparedness in some of the poorest developing countries should be of great concern since they are the most vulnerable to disasters and the least able to handle their own relief without external assistance. The United Nations has identified the least developed countries of the world (LDCs) and those most seriously affected (MSAs) by international economic crisis.(9) "Least developed countries" is a more general category for the poorest of the developing world, while the "most seriously affected" suffer special problems in addition to being an LDC. The MSAs are

> ...those which are at the greatest disadvantage in the world economy; the least developed, the land-locked and other low-income developing countries as well as other developing countries whose economies have been seriously dislocated as a result of the present economic crisis, natural calamities, and foreign aggression and occupation.(10)

Table 3.1 illustrates the levels of disaster preparedness among the combined list of LDC and MSA countries.

Eighty-four percent of these countries have experienced major disasters requiring international assistance within the past five years. Of those countries for which information is available, 43 percent have some form of national disaster organization and only 37 percent have some kind of national disaster plan. Over one-third (37 percent) of the countries which have disaster organizations have no specified plan for action.(11)

Table 3.1.   Disaster Preparedness in the Poorest Countries

National Disaster Plans and National Disaster Organizations*

Afghanistan	India	Pakistan
Bangladesh	Laos	Sri Lanka
Ethiopia	Madagascar	Upper Volta
Honduras	Mauritania	

National Disaster Plans Only

Egypt
El Salvador
Haiti

National Disaster Organizations Only

Chad	Senegal
Mali	Western Samoa
Niger	

No National Plans or National Organizations

Benin	Ghana	Malawi
Botswana	Guinea	Maldives
Burma	Guyana	Nepal
Burundi	Kampuchea, Dem.	Somalia
Cameroon	Kenya	Tanzania
Central African Emp.	Lesotho	Uganda

---

*Country has a full-time standing organization as a disaster focal point, even if only an office or skeleton.

Source: Catholic Relief Services, League of Red Cross Societies, Lutheran World Federation, OXFAM and World Council of Churches, "When Disaster Strikes: A Guide to National   Disaster   Preparedness   in   Disaster-Prone   Areas," Geneva 1976.   Supplemented by information from USAID/FDA Country Profiles.

There is only very limited evidence to suggest that the governments which have instituted disaster preparedness programs have responded in a qualitatively different way from those which have not instituted such programs. In the case of the earthquake in China, the Chinese government refused all offers of outside assistance. China's emphasis on self-sufficiency was mirrored by the governments of Mexico and the Philippines in their responses to subsequent disasters. Precise information of this nature is very difficult to gather due to the basically incomparable nature of disasters. There are too many factors involved in disaster preparedness to make conclusive statements about the nature and extent of improved capacity to handle disaster. However, there is no question about the validity and benefits of an extensive preparedness program for vulnerable countries.

The prerequisites for a successful disaster preparedness program include an interest on the part of the country at risk, a realization that there is a common need for such a program, the scale of the program must be commensurate with the disaster hazard, and the degree of sophistication must be appropriate for the population concerned. There have been numerous activities in recent years which demonstrate an interest in disaster preparedness and a realization of a need to institute such measures. Apart from the activities of UNDRO and other United Nations bodies, groups like the International Congress on Disaster Medicine, the International Civil Defense Organization, the United States Agency for International Development, and many others have conducted numerous seminars on the problems of disaster preparedness.

In many of these countries, disaster hazards have been intensively studied. Many of these countries have received "expert" advice on various aspects of disaster preparedness. Many have sent representatives to attend seminars on the subject. Some of these countries have even received external assistance in establishing disaster plans. But there is still a problem in implementing these plans. Some of the problems facing these countries in instituting disaster preparedness programs have been discussed earlier. The lack of implementation might be partially due to the fact that disaster preparedness and relief coordination at the national level too often represent a partial assignment of officials with several "hats." However, there are a number of factors regarding the nature of international assistsance which also has prohibited the development of preparedness strategies.

First of all, some of the so-called "expert" advice that these countries have received has been inapppropriate. Efforts have been made to impose a general formula for the solution of these problems. A general approach has not worked. Disaster preparedness must be seen in relation to the kind of disaster which is likely to happen and to the potential risk. Not every country is equally exposed to disasters and measures which may be suitable for preparedness in one country may be totally unsatisfactory in another. In addition, preparedness must be adapted to the administrative, technical, organizational and economic conditions of the country concerned. There is little use in establishing a very sophisticated system of disaster preparedness in a country which has no possibility of ever applying it.

Secondly, there has been little follow-up on this advice by these disaster-prone countries. In addition, UNDRO has not been able to provide adequate resources to implement the recommendations proposed by its technical advisory missions. Similarly, the United States Agency for International Development's Office of Foreign Disaster Assistance also is restricted in the amount of assistance that can be offered for implementation.

Advance planning offers a wide range of potential benefits for the economic and social development of disaster-prone countries. It also offers opportunities for the United Nations system to mobilize quickly for disaster relief operations should the need arise. The pre-disaster preparedness plans now being instituted by several disaster-prone developing countries have important implications for the United Nations system and the international community in general.

The major obstacles to better preparedness are not the lack of early warning information or planning techniques, but political unwillingness or administrative inability to use it. The United Nations agencies can contribute to minimizing these obstacles by modifying their traditional short-term relief approach to disaster operations, and becoming involved with encouraging countries to adopt a self-reliant approach to disaster preparedness. For many poor countries with very limited resources to spend on disaster, investments in pre-disaster planning have potential benefits far exceeding those of relief operations mounted after disasters strike. This approach is perhaps the most humane way the international community can demonstrate its concern for the victims of natural disaster.

4 The United Nations and Disaster Preparedness

The most prevalent approach to the problem of natural disasters traditionally has been to send assistance to the victims in the form of relief. Disaster relief also has been the traditional response of the United Nations, which, until very recently, has reacted to disasters only after they occurred. It is grossly inadequate to approach the problem in this way, but some disasters are inevitable and the relief response should be planned in advance.

This chapter will discuss the present state of disaster preparedness within the United Nations. Pre-disaster planning involves a variety of legislative, financial, administrative and organizational arrangements to carry out disaster relief operations. A number of different organizations and programs are involved and collectively comprise the United Nations disaster preparedness strategy. This survey of activities will examine each of the major disaster relief actors in the United Nations system from two perspectives: a) organizational preparedness, and b) the efforts of the organization to promote disaster preparedness in disaster-prone developing countries. While the initiative for instituting disaster preparedness programs clearly lies with the governments of disaster-prone countries, support from the United Nations system of agencies is essential in realizing such change. Therefore, a number of proposals are made for increased United Nations activity in the field of disaster preparedness. These proposals are intended to assess and to explore the financial and other resources which might facilitate greater involvement.

In order to be effective, a United Nations disaster preparedness and relief strategy must underlie all elements of the system and be an integral part of national development planning. At present, the disaster preparedness activities of the different United Nations organizations are not coordinated in any way. The following sections discuss the different roles each organization plays in relief, the possibility for expanded involvement in preparedness, and proposals for a coordinated United Nations approach.

THE UNITED NATIONS CHILDREN'S FUND (UNICEF)

The United Nations Children's Fund was established in 1946 as an emergency relief agency to assist children and adolescents of countries which were victims of war. Since 1950, however, its major objective has been long-range assistance directed at the provision of basic services for children in developing countries. Despite this emphasis on long-range development programs, UNICEF continued to be the major United Nations specialized agency involved in disaster relief during the 1950s.(1)   Since that time, a number of other United Nations bodies have become involved in emergency assistance, and UNICEF has become only one participant in a much larger United Nations system-wide relief effort.

UNICEF has a unique role to play in meeting the special needs of children, which are not always understood or are neglected within the context of an overall relief effort. The basic policy for UNICEF emergency assistance, established by the Executive Board in 1974, has an emphasis on restoration and rehabilitation of basic services infrastructure and long-term programs, rather than emergency aid. Despite this emphasis, UNICEF does have an important role to play in disaster relief.

UNICEF envisions the scope of its emergency services encompassing two general phases: the immediate emergency period; and restoration and rehabilitation, when the interests of other donors have waned. Immediate relief services often take the form of blankets, tents, tarpaulins, special foods for children, vaccine, drugs, and transport. The organization has an operational capacity to procure, deliver and assist governments in combating logistical problems encountered in the delivery of relief supplies. It is capable of generating additional assistance through public appeals, primarily collected by a network of UNICEF National Committees and special appeals to governments and other donors. Aid is provided by UNICEF in disaster situations by diverting suitable regular program supplies available in-country, when a first injection of relief is needed while more extensive aid is being mobilized or when the special needs of children are not sufficiently provided for in the context of the general relief effort.

A stockpile of supplies and transport commonly required in emergencies, such as vehicles (Landrovers), medicines, surgical supplies, special children's food, blankets, cooking and shelter material are kept in the UNICEF Packing and Assembly Center (UNIPAC) in Copenhagen. The items included in this stockpile have been selected as a result of UNICEF's and other organizations' experience in emergency and relief operations.

In the event of a disaster, UNICEF field staff are responsible for alerting headquarters of the emergency. UNICEF staff in a disaster-stricken country generally participate with the government in an assessment of the emergency needs of mothers and children. Following this assessment, and working closely with United Nations agency representatives, an identification of needs is made and a request for assistance is submitted by the government.

The UNICEF Field Manual points out two general reasons why it is not always possible to receive a formal, timely and accurate government request for disaster relief assistance. First of all, there is often a continuing reluctance on the part of responsible ministries of government to seek outside assistance when suddenly faced with a disaster, or when the facts of a creeping disaster emerge. Secondly, a government often does not have a viable agency or interministerial body responsible for relief operations. The result in such situations is that the ministry normally having responsibility for external aid is expected to prepare and submit the formal request for disaster relief. However, such ministries are often concerned with long-term development, and their working procedures may not permit the submission of relief requests quickly.(2) Following a request, UNICEF field representatives are authorized to spend $25,000 or divert supplies and equipment already in-country up to this amount without reference to UNICEF headquarters. Since 1975, all of this activity has been coordinated through the office of the Coordinator of Emergency Operations at UNICEF headquarters, which has been specifically established for this purpose.

The Coordinator of Emergency Operations is, in the event of an emergency, responsible for ensuring coordination between involved field offices and the supporting UNICEF headquarters divisions. He is also responsible for maintaining effective working relationships with concerned United Nations agencies and organizations and other involved bilateral, voluntary and nongovernmental agencies.

Field representatives are expected to establish an information exchange with the Coordinator and keep him informed on all contacts made with donor country representatives.

In addition, the UNICEF Supply Divison has assigned a specific officer for emergency activity, coordination, liaison and follow-up, ensuring that priority status is maintained throughout emergency procurement and shipment.

Arising out of UNICEF's experience in recent disasters, a

flexible emergency financing pattern has evolved. There are actually six different ways to finance relief and rehabilitation under UNICEF's procedures:

- a)   Diversion of supplies and funds from regular country projects to a total value not exceeding $25,000, without reference to headquarters;
- b)   Release from the Executive Director's Emergency Fund established at one million dollars per calendar year;
- c)   "Borrowing" from the commitment for long-term assistance projects under special conditions and with headquarters approval;
- d)   Transfers from the commitments for long-term assistance projects with headquarters approval;
- e)   Special contributions by donor governments and others as a result of appeals; and
- f)   Executive Board commitments made specifically for the relief and rehabilitation assistance upon the recommendation of the Executive Director. (3)

UNICEF has made a number of internal changes in recent years which have increased its organizational preparedness to a great degree. The preparedness of UNICEF personnel is an ongoing task. Along this line, UNICEF's Emergency Operrations Office participates in field personnel orientation where the administrative arrangements regarding disaster relief procedures are discussed.

While UNICEF recognizes the importance of its own organizational preparedness, it emphasizes that, "More important than the preparedness of international agencies, countries need a nucleus of key organizational arrangements and personnel to deal with emergencies."(4) In disaster-prone developing countries, UNICEF has helped to establish permanent disaster coordination machinery after it has been set up for a particular disaster, as in Haiti. UNICEF is also involved in a joint FAO/WHO/UNICEF project on nutritional surveillance. In Ethiopia there is a food-monitoring pilot project which is supported by UNICEF. Despite these efforts, there have been too few projects with similar disaster preparedness objectives.

Because UNICEF offers very unique and specialized services within the spectrum of disaster relief assistance, there also would appear to be a number of unique and special ways in which UNICEF could promote disaster preparedness in developing countries. With this in mind, the following suggestions are offered as ways in which UNICEF could more actively contribute to disaster preparedness:

1) UNICEF should designate disaster preparedness as a priority activity in its development programs.

2) The Coordinator of Emergency Operations should be responsible for directing and co-ordinating a comprehensive disaster prepared-ness strategy separate from, but coordinated with, the country programs.

3) Increased attention should be given to disaster relief education of UNICEF personnel both through orientation and in-service training.

4) Training of national personnel in disaster-prone countries in emergency child care should be a priority disaster preparedness program.

5) Research should be conducted to develop ideas for specific projects that UNICEF could assist that would improve the current preparedness posture of disaster-prone member states.

Disaster preparedness education of UNICEF personnel should be an ongoing activity which should be imparted to field personnel in more innovative ways than lecture orientation. For example, regional in-service training seminars and disaster preparedness exercises might be instituted to insure that relief procedures are operational, and not just a "paper plan" which is taken out for reference when a disaster occurs.

UNICEF also can help in national preparedness and in training programs for emergency child care. This area of activity needs to be emphasized much more than it is at the present time. The training of personnel is an important feature of disaster relief preparedness, and the care of children in a disaster, particularly their health needs, often requires special education not available through regular development programs.

UNICEF has a policy of funding applied research, which is directed to solving field problems of services benefiting children and to enhancing the value of UNICEF aid. This avenue of endeavor could produce studies, pilot projects and surveys, demonstrating the potential benefits of a disaster preparedness program, as well as generating specific ideas for projects in identified areas and countries.

One avenue of funds for a disaster preparedness program might be the annual pledging conference. Annual pledging conferences began in November 1974, when a special pledging conference was convened by the General Assembly. In December of that year, the General Assembly endorsed the Executive Board's declaration of an emergency for children in developing countries and requested that the Secretary-General convene regular annual pledging conferences starting

in 1975.(5)   At the pledging conferences, several governments
have announced contributions for specific purposes in addition
to their pledges for UNICEF general resources.   In preparing
for future pledging conferences, the letter and memorandum
introducing UNICEF's current orientation or assistance should
specifically mention disaster preparedness as a priority
program area.

UNICEF, with its experience in relief and its operational
capacity, could play a vital role in preparing disaster-prone
countries to handle the special needs of mothers and children
when disaster strikes.   While it is recognized that UNICEF
cannot design projects of its own choosing, and that the
organization deals with sovereign independent governments
which must ultimately choose their own paths to development,
UNICEF can advocate, advise and promote disaster preparedness through its discussions and negotiations with various
ministries.   This requires a fundamental awareness on the part
of the field representative of potential disaster hazards, past
disaster relief performance, problems encountered, and the
potential benefits to be gained from a comprehensive
preparedness program.

THE FOOD AND AGRICULTURE ORGANIZATION (FAO)
AND THE WORLD FOOD PROGRAMME (WFP)

The provision of food in a disaster relief situation has
always been a primary concern.   It has been estimated that 80
percent of all relief provided in natural disasters is food.(6)
Much of the criticism which has arisen over the past several
years of the United Nations disaster relief operations has
centered around the provision and distribution of food.(7)
There are many reasons for this criticism because food is a
bulk commodity and the delivery of large supplies of food,
particularly grain, is a very complex operation.   Accusations
have been made that food relief which might continue in-
definitely such as when a drought occurs, destroys the local
incentive to produce and store food.   Since many problems of
emergency food aid distribution could be alleviated by
planning, a concerted effort toward preparing for food relief
operations should be made.

The Food and Agriculture Organization

The Food and Agriculture Organization has been involved
in disaster assistance since 1951, when the FAO Conference
first discussed its role in meeting emergency food needs in
disaster situations.   The procedure employed by FAO was as

follows: When notice was received from a member state or region that a serious food shortage or famine existed or was likely to develop, and it was unable to cope with the situation from its own resources, the Director-General sent FAO officials to investigate. A report on the extent of international assistance that was needed was sent to the United Nations and interested specialized agencies. If, in the opinion of the Director-General, there existed an emergency requiring international relief measures, he could, at his discretion, convene a meeting of representatives of interested governments. Action to assist the affected government would be proposed and taken to the Secretary-General for transmission to the Economic and Social Council (ECOSOC).

As early as 1952, ECOSOC recommended that preparatory arrangements be made by governments which might be subject to famine emergencies. It was further recommended that FAO develop a system of famine detection and that famine emergency relief activities be coordinated by the Secretary-General. (8)

By the beginning of the 1960s, FAO had had considerable experience with large-scale food assistance operations. Under the influence of the FAO Principles of Surplus Disposal and other reflections of international opinion and experience, the motive for this assistance had changed from the experience and opportunism of surplus disposal and agricultural export promotion to assisting in the development of the poorer countries. By 1966, this change has reached the point of firm emphasis (at least in theory) on the concept that food aid should actively promote, and not discourage, agricultural development and nutritional self-sufficiency in the developing countries. Actually, food aid was used for many purposes and had diverse effects. In 1963, the World Food Programme was established. A sum of US$7 million of the Programme's resources was reserved during the initial period every year for the use of the Director-General of FAO to meet emergency needs. This amount was increased to US$45 million in 1977.

Disaster-related assistance is not restricted to food, as FAO also responds to requests for rehabilitation aid in the agricultural sector of a disaster-stricken country. Its emergency services involve aid in the restoration of seeds, provision of pesticides and other factors relating to productivity, rather than the provision of emergency supplies.

In the late 1960s, the ability of FAO to respond was challenged by the increasing demands of drought-stricken populations in the Sahel and Ethiopia. The continuing drought in the Sahel reached its most disastrous proportions in 1973-74. In response to this crisis, the Office for Sahelian Relief Operations (OSRO) was created within FAO in 1973, and became the focal point for the entire United Nations relief effort. This office also maintained an active role in the Ethiopian operation and several others that followed.

In 1975, OSRO's mandate was expanded to include emergency operations all over the world which fall within FAO's specific fields of action and OSRO became known as the Office for Special Relief Operations. In this capacity, OSRO provides agricultural input and technical assistance where required for sudden disasters and in emergencies with longer-term consequences. Its activities include recovery programs and similar forms of assistance to facilitate rehabilitation and development. OSRO's operations are based on voluntary contributions from the United Nations system for specific projects which have a direct bearing on increasing food production. This program is an integrated part of FAO's regular program and all segments of the organization are involved in its execution. For the biennium 1978-79, US$4 million was allocated to meet urgent needs related to disaster, or disturbances which affect or are expected to affect a country's food and agricultural situation.

There are a number of other activities of the regular program of FAO which have some relationship to disaster prevention and preparedness - the Global Information and Early Warning System, the World Food Security Assistance Scheme, the Global Nutritional Surveillance System, the International Fertilizer Supply Scheme, the Desert Locust Control Program, the World Livestock Disease Reporting Scheme and the Remote Sensing Unit. Of these schemes, three information systems - the Global Nutritional Surveillance System, the Global Information and Early Warning System and the World Food Security Assistance Scheme - have been established since 1974 as a result of World Food Conference recommendations.

The World Food Conference recommended that a Global Nutritional Surveillance System be established by FAO, UNICEF, and WHO. The purpose of this program is to provide technical assistance to countries to set up their own national nutritional surveillance systems. The system is intended to "monitor the food and nutrition conditions of the disadvantaged groups of the population at risk, and to provide a method of rapid and permanent assessment of all factors which influence food consumption patterns and nutritional status."(9) While this sounds simple enough at the outset, the relationships between weather, crops, food prices, consumption and health are very complex and not easily predicted. With regard to describing the progression of a population towards famine, the problems of prediction are equally difficult. As one writer has suggested, "...what distinguishes a famine from a food shortage is a relatively sudden breakdown in economic and social relations which is neither preceded by clear trends nor easily measured by indicators."(10) So far, several countries have tried to establish national surveillance programs (e.g., Ethiopia, Bangladesh, Kenya, Tanzania, the Philippines, Upper Volta). Despite reservations about the reliability of the methodology involved, this system does represent a solid commitment to disaster preparedness.

The Global Information and Early Warning System was established in 1974, following a recommendation of the World Food Conference. There are now 90 participating countries cooperating in this information exchange. The purpose of this program is to

> monitor continuously the world food supply and demand conditions so as to assist government to plan ahead; to identify countries or regions where serious food shortages and worsening nutritional conditions are imminent; and to contribute to the effective functioning of the international undertaking on World Food Security.(11)

Technical assistance is also being provided to a number of developing countries in strengthening or setting up national early warning systems. The sources of information of the system are the participating governments, FAO and WFP representatives in the countries concerned, other United Nations field staff, press, radio, and news wire services. The system is not responsible for follow-up action, but it makes every effort to ensure that action is taken by the appropriate units or agencies.

The World Food Security Assistance Scheme was established in April 1976, as a result of a World Food Conference recommendation. Thus far, 74 of FAO's member states and the European Economic Community (EEC) have adhered to this scheme, whose purpose is to promote cooperative action by governments to avoid acute food shortages in the event of widespread crop failures or natural disasters. The establishment of national food security policies such as national grain reserves and other programs related to food security like storage construction and stock conservation is an essential feature of disaster preparedness. The scheme also provides for missions, particularly to disaster-prone areas, in order to assist governments in the elaboration of long-term food reserve projects.

The International Fertilizer Supply Scheme has been operating since 1973, and has alerted the world to the disastrous consequences of fertiziler shortages. The scheme is instrumental in mobilizing financial resources in cases of need, and in improving domestic production of fertilizer in developing countries.

The purpose of the Desert Locust Control Program is to detect and destroy locusts before they achieve a plague status. This is accomplished through careful surveying of the breeding areas and timely control of the incipient population. A network of wireless stations is used to transmit information rapidly. The application of satellite remote sensing techniques is at an experimental stage. The programs are largely financed by participating governments.

It is hoped that all of these interrrelated information systems will have a considerable impact on the future disater preparedness capabilities of developing countries. Despite these notable efforts, emphasis should be placed on developing a comprehensive and coordinated strategy of disaster preparedness within FAO.

The following activities are offered as suggestions for FAO's participation in disaster preparedness:

1) FAO should make disaster preparedness an important development activity, identify needs and priorities and target goals for achievement.

2) OSRO should encourage member states to develop special preparedness projects in the agricultural sector as an integrated part of rural development.

3) A portion of the extra-budgetary funds available to FAO for emergency assistance should be set aside as a subaccount for disaster preparedness.

4) FAO's strategy for disaster preparedness should include organizing local skills, mobilizing local initiative, talent and resources.

5) As the focal point for special relief operations, OSRO should be responsible for directing and coordinating FAO's disaster preparedness program.

6) OSRO should become involved in the orientation of FAO personnel, which should include presentations involving: a) disaster awareness; b) administrative arrangements for relief situations within FAO and with other United Nations agencies; and c) discussions on ways to promote disaster preparedness within the longer-term agricultural development program of a country.

7) OSRO should initiate an in-service training preparedness program for disaster relief.

Agricultural preparedness for disaster should have a built-in evaluation system to determine whether the targeted groups are really benefiting and the methods and skills taught are appropriate, given the types of disaster needs. FAO, through its Office for Special Relief Operations, should take the lead in defining the ways in which this can be accomplished most effectively.

The World Food Programme

The United Nations and FAO jointly established the World Food Programme in 1963 for an initial three-year experimental period in order to channel food surpluses to needy countries for development purposes. Since that time, WFP has become an important multilateral resources program which mobilizes the food production potential of donor countries in order to generate additional development resources for recipient countries (supplementing capital aid and technical assistance). While the major emphasis of WFP is on development assistance through food aid, the Programme has met a significant amount of emergency food needs throughout the years.

Among the United Nations organizations, WFP disposes of the largest amount of resources for disaster relief. From 1963 to 1973, 15 percent of WFP's total expenditure was disbursed as aid in emergencies ($110.9 million). This ranged from a low of $1.6 million in 1965, to a high of $19.3 million in 1970.(12)

In its early years, WFP distributed largely surplus foodstuffs. By 1970, the need for WFP emergency assistance had been growing at a time when WFP's capacity to respond had been decreasing. The Programme had been forced to stretch its emergency assistance by such means as giving lower rations, offering in a number of instances only token assistance, using its expertise in coordinating other donor assistance, and charging relief to food-for-work, rehabilitation and reconstruction-type projects.

As pre-1973 surplus supplies became depleted and WFP's capacity to respond decreased, food shortages became more widespread, the importance of food aid increased, and the costs to donor countries increased. The figure of $10 million, which was set as the annual emergency operations budget, was hardly adequate in view of the fact that prices of major WFP commodities, freight and transportation costs have, on the average, doubled since 1967.(13) For example, between 1972 and 1975 WFP conducted, on the average, 24 emergency operations a year, at an average cost of $34.2 million a year. Since 1975 there have been on the average 26 operations per year, with an average cost of $63.1 million.(14) As can be seen, the $10 million usually proved inadequate in the face of repeated disasters of varying severity.

In response to this crisis, the emergency reserves of food within the regular WFP allocation were increased in 1975 from $10 million annually to $40 million annually, with provision for yearly revision of that allocation.(15) Table 4.1 illustrates the nature and extent of this crisis.

The Programme's resources for emergency aid are made available at the decision of the Director-General of FAO, based on the recommendation of the Executive Director of WFP. Besides the $40 million annual emergency relief budget, the

Table 4.1.   World Food Programme (WFP)
Emergency Operations, 1972-1977
(Amounts Actually Dispersed)

Year	Number of Operations	Value ($US Millions)
1972-73 (June 1972- July 1973)	20	16.9
1973-74 (July 1973- June 1974)	10	9.9
1974-75 (April 1974- March 1975)*	17	18.1
1975-76 (Mar. 1975- Apr. 1976)	40	60.7
(Jan.-Nov. 1976)**	21	38
1977 (Jan.-May 1977)	12	27.5
Total	120	171.1

*The estimate for 1974-75 may be too high, due to an over-accounting of two months.

**The estimate for 1975-76 may be inaccurate because of an overaccounting at the beginning of two months and an under-accounting of two months at the end of the period.   This period reports on activities covering a period of 21 months, accounting for the high number of operations and cost.

Sources: WFP/IGC:24/5-A, August 1973, p. 1; WFP/IGC:26/5-B, September 1974, p. 1; WFP/IGC:27/18, April 1975, p. 2; WFP/CFA:1/21, June 1976, p. 4; WFP/CFA:2/19, December 1976, pp. 4-5; Annual Report of the Committee on Food Aid Policies and Programmes, June 14, 1977 (5/6008), pp. 4-5.

International Emergency Food Reserve is also available.   First
recommended in 1975 by the United Nations General Assembly,
the purpose of this reserve is to provide a quantity of 500,000
tons of food stocks, or the equivalent funds, to use in disaster relief situations and other emergencies.   In 1976, $8
million was drawn from this fund for emergency relief
purposes.(16)

      The Emergency Unit in the Project Management Division
was established in 1975 by WFP's governing body, the Committee on Food Aid Policies and Programmes.   The primary
function of the Emergency Unit is to assess emergency requirements, and coordinate WFP aid with other multilateral and
bilateral food assistance.   Relief supplies from donor countries
include a wide spectrum of commodities ranging from cereals to
canned cheese, meat and fish and dried skim milk.   Apart from
the provision of food, the Emergency Unit must also handle
shipping, insurance, and other expenses involved in getting
foodstuffs from donors to recipients.   The Emergency Unit
sees its activities as falling into two general categories: immediate emergency post-disaster assistance and reconstruction
programmes.   Reconstruction, or one-year agricultural re-
habiliation, programs merit the same importance and
procedures as emergency programs, but do not necessarily
promote future preparedness for relief.   These programs are
designed as an additional measure to insure that the
development process is not interrupted by the disaster.

      WFP also has a role in preventing or forestalling
emergencies which include projects or flood control, soil conservation, land reclamation, canal lining, access roads and
building up of national food reserves.   In cooperation with
other UN agencies, food-for-work projects have been designed
to meet food needs that extend beyond the immediate
emergency period.   Like disaster prevention, disaster preparedness activities such as pre-positioning of food stocks in
disaster-prone areas and food security programs are the
responsibilities of the geographic branches and country desks.
However, the Emergency Unit recognizes its own disaster
preparedness responsibilities with regard to improving WFP's
capacity to coordinate and facilitate the food relief provided by
other donors.

      During a relief operation, a situation report is issued by
the Emergency Unit approximately every two weeks to the
donors involved in the operation.   This reporting is done on
an ad hoc basis as needed.   The report concerns shipping,
port storage and transportation information which is provided
to the service by the donors.   Internal coordination with WFP
headquarters should improve in the future, as a monthly progress report for internal circulation is planned to inform other
branches of relief operations and the Emergency Unit's activities.

With regard to WFP officer training, the Emergency Unit does not participate in any disaster orientation for new field personnel. There are some future plans regarding a field manual for administrative use in emergency food operations, which would assist WFP personnel in acquainting themselves with supply and logistical aspects of food relief operations. There is no program to educate those already in service.

In order to be more active in disaster preparedness, a number of suggestions are posed for additional World Food Programme activities:

1) WFP should make disaster preparedness an important development activity, which could be assisted through food aid.

2) WFP should identify the priorities and needs in disaster preparedness which fall within its areas of special competence, and target goals for achievement.

3) As the focal point for WFP relief activities, the Emergency Unit should be responsible for directing and coordinating WFP's program of disaster preparedness.

4) The Emergency Unit should institute a program of disaster orientation and in-service disaster relief training.

5) The Emergency Unit should become concerned with promoting in disaster-prone countries an awareness of the benefits of planning ahead for an emergency food assistance program, and assist these member states in designing projects relevant to a food relief preparedness strategy.

Summary

The lack of preparedness activities within FAO's Office for Special Relief Operations and the WFP Emergency Unit illustrates a dilemma that other United Nations disaster units have also been facing. What seems to be needed in disaster preparedness is a strategy - an overall approach for the United Nations to adopt - rather than each agency pursuing its own goals. This strategy needs to specify the objectives of diaster preparedness, define the scope of activities within which the United Nations will become involved, and the means by which these activities will be pursued. The underlying premise for a coherent diaster preparedness strategy is a common understanding of the concept and what is involved. The World Food Programme and the Food and Agriculture

Organization, because of their prominent roles in disaster relief, should become more active in defining this strategy.

THE WORLD HEALTH ORGANIZATION (WHO)

The effects of natural disasters on the health of populations are many and diverse. The organization of emergency medical care, whether it be in the disaster-stricken country or provided by an international relief agency, is a critical aspect of any disaster relief organization. In 1948, the First World Health Assembly adopted a program for emergency service and decided that in the case of serious epidemics WHO should be regarded as the "first source of assistance to which countries have recourse."(17) The constitution of the World Health Organization states that its role in emergency health assistance is "to furnish appropriate technical assistance and, in emergencies, necessary aid upon request or acceptance of governments." Over the years WHO assumed the following responsibilities in disaster situations:

a)   The rapid provision of medicaments and other medical supplies needed for the prevention and control of communicable diseases caused or aggravated by the disaster;

b)   The provision of technical advice and approval of all medical equipment and supplies provided by UNICEF, non-governmental organizations and voluntary agencies;

c)   The provision of technical assistance and advice on specific areas of public health, such as drinking water and malnutrition;

d)   Assuring close collaboration with the International Committee of the Red Cross and the Leage of Red Cross Societies, which in different ways play an important role in assisting countries during emergency situations.(18)

In all emergency relief operations WHO is the overall focal point for health and medical assistance irrespective of source, and the Emergency Relief Operations Office acts as the functional center for emergency operations. WHO is also the United Nations agency responsible for providing health assistance at times of disasters caused by toxicity from chemicals, food poisoning and health hazards caused by air pollution, water pollution or by the massive use of insecticides.

Emergencies which are limited to the field of health, such as epidemics or outbreaks of communicable diseases, are handled primarily by WHO through cooperation with the national health authorities and voluntary agencies, including national Red Cross societies.

Great disasters in the early 1970s not only took a great toll of human life (Bangladesh and the Sahel), but were also largely responsible for changes in political systems (Pakistan, Ethiopia, Niger). These disasters provided WHO with the momentum to develop a new strategy in dealing with emergency health care problems. Member states expressed their concern and interest in a more active role for the organization in a series of resolutions.(19)

In May 1974, the World Health Assembly directed WHO to take steps "to meet more readily the urgent needs of countries stricken by disasters or natural catastrophes."(20) The following June the Director-General established the Intra-secretariat Coordination Committee on Early Warning Systems, and in November 1974, an officer in the Division of Co-ordination was designed as Responsible Officer for WHO Emergency Relief Operations.

The following Assembly in May 1975, requested the Director-General "to continue to develop further the Or-ganization's capacity for providing health assistance to disaster-stricken peoples, and to ensure that the Organization continues to play an active role in the joint relief and re-habilitation efforts undertaken by the United Nations system and the League of Red Cross Societies with respect to di-sasters and natural catastrophes."(21) Since July 1975, the Responsible Officer for Emergency Relief Operations has reported directly to the Deputy Director-General, and is thus attached to the Office of the Director-General.

The Responsible Officer for Emergency Relief operations is the chief coordinator of WHO-assisted relief operations and liaison officer on these subjects with other organizations. However, this is not the sole function of this office. The Responsible Officer is the liaison officer for WHO with the national liberation movements recognized by the Organization for African Unity (OAU). This part of the responsibilities of this office takes up almost half the normal working day.

The WHO disaster relief officer is assisted by a six-member advisory panel, whose members are called upon in-dividually to recommend specific technical advice. However, it is not clear whether these individuals have the authority to speak for their divisions. Other than these advisors, who have their regular responsibilities in addition to their disaster relief advisory duties, the disaster relief officer has only two secretarial assistants, one financed by the regular budget and the other by extra-budgetary resources. A disaster medical officer has also been added to the staff, and the services of

the Medical Supplies Unit are at the disposal of the Emergency
Relief Operations office for processing and supplying
emergency medicaments and supplies in disaster situations.
WHO's fund for disaster relief activities is the Special
Account for Disaster and Natural Catastrophes of the
Voluntary Fund for Health Promotion, which was established in
1975. This account enables the organization to act as a donor
in a disaster relief situation rather than as a donor's assistant. It is a significant, but until now a mostly symbolic,
development in the disaster funding strategy. During the
first year of the fund's experience only $55,000 was allotted
for the disaster account. Practically all of the funds that WHO
spends in procuring medical supplies for disaster-stricken
governments come from trusts provided by donor governments
or from the United Nations system. A $20,000 limit for each
disaster has been used as a guideline. A further factor affecting the accessibility of the disaster account has been to
limit its use to the procurement of medical supplies.
WHO assisted in 17 different disaster relief operations
during the period 1971-1975. In at least half of the operations, it was necessary to send WHO staff to the disaster-
stricken area to assist the local health officials. The WHO
respresentative in a disaster-prone country has the responsibility of advising the government on the need for establishing a system which ensures the early assessment of the
health situation and needs in disaster-prone areas. In 1974,
field representatives were given the authority to offer assistance immediately in investigating the outbreak of a disease.
Information concerning emergency relief operations is sent
directly to the Responsible Officer of Emergency Relief
Operations Office at Geneva Headquarters. Regional offices
are involved primarily as channels for relief supplies and as
advisors to headquarters.
In addition to disaster relief, WHO is at present spon-
soring research in the field of disaster science. Arrangements
are under way to train Fellows with the aim of creating a
nucleus of trained personnel who will teach others and
carry out research as well as operational tasks. Constant
efforts to prepare for disasters are essential, and given the
responsibilities of WHO in medical relief, it is only fitting that
WHO play an active role in medical preparedness. In order to
understand more fully the importance of preparedness in the
health sector, it is necessary to appreciate the relationship
between disasters and disease.

Disasters and Disease

Contrary to common belief, disasters are not necessarily
followed by major epidemics. Famine is an exception to this

statement, but in any area where malnutrition is prevalent, the population has an increased susceptibility to, and mortality from, infectious diseases. In much of the developing world, the occurrence of disease following a disaster is a serious problem. In some cases, communicable diseases may cause more death than the primary disaster, but this is not caused by the disaster itself, but rather by social disruption. crowding in refugee camps, deficient sanitation, and trauma which follow disasters.

One of the most common mistakes made in the health sector following a disaster is to institute mass vaccination campaigns. As one expert in the field of disaster epidemiology has said:

> The general attitude to disaster is that they are inescapably linked with epidemics. There is pressure to vaccinate against all kinds of diseases.(22)

Mass immunization against typhoid fever is widely practiced in disaster situations, especially after floods, but the usefulness of this practice has never been evaluated. In the Managua earthquake in 1972 over a million doses of typhoid vaccine were sent to the affected area by donor countries and voluntary agencies. Contrary to the instructions of the health authorities, a quarter of a million doses were injected. The result of these procedures was to divert useful and badly needed personnel from more important activities and to run the risk of increasing the incidence of hepatitis.(23) In addition, no provision was made to identify persons for a second and third shot, rendering the entire effort meaningless.

Communicable diseases pose a secondary threat in almost every disaster situation, but the risk of an outbreak of communicable disease of epidemic proportion is grossly exaggerated. Even in less developed countries, classical diseases such as smallpox, plague, typhus and malaria have disappeared or have become severely restricted in their distribution. Experience of the World Health Organization in several large disasters since 1966 indicates that serious outbreaks of communicable diseases have not occurred.(24) However, disasters can increase the transmission of disease in the region in the following circumstances:

1) Impact of the disaster. The disaster itself may cause contamination of the water and food supply and increase the risk of vector-transmitted diseases like malaria.

2) Overcrowding and poor sanitation in refugee camps. The overcrowding of large populations, contamination of food, water and the camp environment may lead to an outbreak of communicable diseases. This is particularly true when a nu-

tritional emergency already exists and the population is weakened by malnutrition. Drought and the resulting famine is a natural disaster most commonly associated with disease. For example, following the civil war in Bangladesh in 1971, there were epidemics of smallpox and cholera. This was primarily due to the lack of basic sanitation facilities. Examples of natural disasters which may potentially harm the water supply are earthquakes, floods and cyclones. Detection of contaminated water may reflect a permanent problem rather than a temporary one resulting from the disaster event. After the Guatemala earthquake in 1976, costly measures were taken to ensure the provision of a minimum supply of safe water. Daily bacteriological and chemical analyses were made of the main system in Guatemala City, while other areas had to depend on the emergency airlifting of 3,000-gallon rubberized tankers (at a cost of US$850 per flying hour). While this may not seem a reasonable way to tackle problems of this kind, among 18 remote sites surveyed only one village reported a lack of water. This result suggests that because of the action taken, water supply did not constitute a major disaster-associated health problem.(25)

3)   Disruption of ongoing disease control programs.   The disease which is targeted for eradication may recur as a result of the control program being disrupted, not because of the disaster. The Nigerian civil war completely disrupted the leprosy treatment program. The war also delayed the mass smallpox/measles immunization campaign for almost two years. Another case is that of malaria in 1963, following hurricane Flora. Flora caused extensive damage to housing with about 68 percent of the houses destroyed and most of the roofs blown away. This occurred in the course of an extensive malaria eradication campaign and flushed away the residual insecticide which had been sprayed on the walls of the dwellings. A severe malaria epidemic developed six to eight weeks after the hurricane with an estimated 75,000 cases.(26) An effort is usually made by WHO to utilize the disaster as an opportunity to introduce a more balanced medium-term health programming in the rehabilitation phase.

WHO has long recognized the importance of controlling disaster-related disease, and has taken some steps toward preparing for relief operations. WHO has established a sim-plified short list of essential drugs which can be produced more easily and cheaply. Likewise, it has collaborated with the League of Red Cross Societies in establishing a list of essential medicaments and supplies in case of disaster. WHO and UNDRO have arranged to transport relief supplies at advantageous rates and WHO has arranged to purchase drugs and supplies for emergencies at a much reduced cost.

The primary role of WHO in disaster preparedness in

developing countries is confined to providing the necessary technical and administrative advice in assisting governments to develop their own preparedness programs. Funding for these programs must compete with longer-term development priorities. The Emergency Operations Office has no available funds to enable the organization to carry out these responsibilities. Outside this office, the individual technical divisions each have their own preparedness programs for emergency assistance, but disaster preparedness is variously interpreted according to the particular area of activity involved. There has been no attempt to coordinate or exchange information in order to develop an overall preparedness strategy. However, recent interest in one of the regional offices of WHO has led to a more active involvement in disaster preparedness as a specialized and separate program.

Disaster Preparedness - Pan American Health Organization (PAHO)

Since 1947, the Pan American Sanitary Bureau has been the regional office for the Americas of the World Health Organization known as the Pan American Health Organization (PAHO). The organization provides advice and technical assistance to help its 31 member governments to expand health services, make better use of community resources and solve specific health problems. Among these problems are emergencies and disaster situations.

The Americas are particularly vulnerable to natural disasters. Since 1970, over 100,000 people living in Latin America or the Caribbean have lost their lives because of natural disaster - 70,000 alone died in the Peruvian earthquake in 1970; 10,000 died in the Nicaraguan earthquake in 1972; and 23,000 died in 1976 in the Guatemalan earthquake. Concern over the vulnerability of the Americas to disasters led to some decisive action on the part of PAHO to upgrade its disaster relief assistance.

In the past, disaster relief assistance from PAHO consisted of providing specialized medical supplies or equipment and technical assistance on specific public health problems such as the prevention of outbreaks of communicable disease, establishment of an emergency potable water supply, water control, and the restoration of medical services. This traditional assistance had limited impact on emergency preparedness planning and international relief efforts.

In October 1976, the Directing Council of PAHO requested the director to set up a disaster unit with instructions to define the policy of the Organization, to formulate a plan of action for the various types of disasters, to make an inventory of the human and other resources available, to train the necessary personnel, to prepare and disseminate the appropriate guidelines and manuals, and to promote operational research to meet the needs of the countries in disaster situations, and to insure that this unit establish effective coordination with the United Nations Disaster Relief Co-ordinator, the International Red Cross, and other national and international bodies providing disaster assistance.(27)

In March 1977, a permanent unit for Emergency Preparedness and Disaster Relief Coordination was established at PAHO headquarters in Washington, D.C. There are three major areas of activity in which the Emergency Unit is engaged:

1) Preparation of PAHO to respond to an emergency in a member country. A roster is being compiled of PAHO staff and other experts available for short-term assignments in case of emergencies, and emergency administrative procedures (e.g., procurement, recruitment) are being formulated.
2) Emergency preparedness in member states. Technical asssistance is provided upon request from the countries. This technical assistance may take the form of seminars, workshops, short-term advisory service, information exchange and the like. In 1976, a multinational seminar was held in Guatemala on the subject of public health management during emergencies; guidelines are being prepared by PAHO as a result of the recommendations of this seminar. This guide will outline the concepts of disaster management and summarizes recent knowledge in disaster epidemiology.
3. Training and research. PAHO is currently studying the feasibility of providing field training during actual emergencies for its staff as well as for national counterpart personnel. In addition, PAHO is planning to sponsor research concerning disaster operations. Grants to research institutions might be activated at the time of an emergency, allowing the researcher on-the-spot coverage of the aftermath of a disaster.

PAHO's disaster relief assistance is financed in two ways. First, is the Emergency Revolving Fund, which is available for the immediate financing of emergency relief supplies. Its use is subject to a commitment by the receiving government to reimburse the fund as soon as possible. A second way is the National Disaster Relief Voluntary Fund, established in 1976, which finances: a) the provisions of essential relief supplies, and b) technical assistance in carrying out a realistic as-

sessment of the relief needs and in improving national management and cooperation of international assistance. This fund
has resources of approximately $100,000.

The funds for preparedness activities are very limited.
In 1979, a disaster preparedness fund may be established for
the specific purpose of assisting member countries in their
planning for future relief operations. PAHO is also considering an emergency reserve for its field officers to be used
in the event of disaster, similar to the arrangement that now
exists for UNICEF and UNDP field staff.

It is most likely that PAHO will continue to be the only
WHO regional office with a special Emergency Unit for a long
time. It requires substantial resources to establish such an
office and a serious commitment to disaster preparedness
requires serious financial expenditures.

Emergency Health Care Preparedness in Developing Countries

The answer to more effective management of emergency
health care in times of disaster seems to lie in disaster preparedness planning. As recommended by two leading scholars
in the field of disaster epidemiology:

> By re-thinking the problem today, (their)
> decisions in case of tomorrow's disaster are likely to
> be more effective. Disaster preparedness is not a
> matter of pouring money into field hospitals and
> technology, but in laying down the foundation for a
> realistic assessment of immediate and long-term
> needs in times of mass emergencies.(28)

In the health sector, the primary preparedness needs of
disaster-prone developing countries focus upon three general
areas: organization, training, and operations.

Organization

The top public health official in the region or country
should be responsible for coordinating emergency health care
preparedness. Sometimes the national emergency committee
assumes this responsibility. Whether this coordination and
direction is taken by a committee or by the office of the
ministry of health, the strategy should be comprehensive in
linking all levels of health administration.(29)

Inadequate disaster planning has been identified as one of
the major problems facing health administrators. Karl A.
Western points out that even in a developed country like the
United States with an advanced health care system, only the

"75 percent of hospitals which are accredited have disaster plans."(30) Even when hospital disaster plans do exist, they often fail because they exist only on paper. They are either poorly conceived or not practiced frequently enough to be implemented effectively when needed. Disaster plans may either be too specific or too general, or deviate from standard operating procedures. A written plan is worthless unless it is functional and operational.

Training

Medical personnel in developing countries, unless the country has had frequent disasters, may not have been involved in disaster before, may not have had any formal training in disaster medicine, and may lack the discipline and support systems to withstand the disruption of services following a disaster. Medical facilities in developing countries may be very rudimentary, and may not be designed to handle either mass casualties or the special needs (i.e., psychological) of a disaster-stricken population. In normal times, medical and laboratory facilities may be inadequate for the diagnosis of epidemic diseases such as smallpox, cholera, and typhoid with any great degree of consistency or assurance, but conditions will be worse after a disaster.

Operations

A major part of emergency health care preparedness is to appreciate the patterns of injuries that occur as a result of different kinds of disasters. For example, it is not unusual for landslides and avalanches to result in no survivors. The same excess of deaths take place in volcanic eruptions, tsunamis and floods.(31) These facts must be taken into consideration when planning for the number of medical personnel to be trained for emergency health care, the number and kind of specialists, and the amount and kind of emergency medical supplies to be stored or requested.

An example of a successful attempt to improve a nutritional relief program took place in May 1974 in Niger, and was sponsored by the government of Niger, the League of Red Cross Societies and the United Nations Development Programme. The goal of the project was to examine the human nutritional status of a selected population as a basis for making administrative decisions on priorities in the distribution of relief and the location of medical teams. The report of this program recommended that an assessment and evaluation system should be built in and budgeted in any major nutritional relief program and performed by local health workers rather than by an expatriate team.(32)

Diverse opinions exist concerning the advisability and

usefulness of establishing stockpiles of emergency medical supplies. However, the task of assessing the medical needs of a disaster-stricken population and formulating requests for international aid can be made much simpler if records are kept, and constantly updated, of emergency medical supplies available in the country.

The operational aspects of caring for disaster victims could be made more effective through better management techniques and adequate training of medical personnel, but there must exist a disaster plan of emergency health care for the entire country. Identifying the nature and scope of a population's vulnerability to disaster and initiating programs to combat this vulnerability and to care for this population when disaster strikes should be the goal of WHO-assisted disaster preparedness programs.

Disaster relief operations are conditioned by what was or was not planned before the disaster. Post-disaster evaluations of the relief response can reveal deficiencies and propose alternative methods to improve future relief operations. In addition, what is needed to improve an organization's disaster assistance capability are scientific studies to discover ways of applying scientific and technical knowledge to disaster prevention, preparedness and mitigation.

Preparedness for WHO Officials

The initiation of a disaster preparedness function for the WHO Emergency Relief Operation Office could prove invaluable to the field and regional offices, which are currently responsible for disaster rehabilitation assistance. A 1975 management survey recommended that headquarters should be responsible for disaster relief and that the regional offices should be responsible for rehabilitation assistance, with both sides assisting each other.(33) However, disaster preparedness programs are difficult to classify as they are neither relief nor rehabilitation. The implementation and design of emergency health preparedness programs must be integrated into the medium- and long-term health needs of a country and should therefore be entrusted to regional offices. However, there is clearly an important role that the Responsible Office for Emergency Relief Operations at headquarters could play in promoting these programs, in coordinating these efforts at the headquarters level, and ensuring that disaster preparedness receives the high priority that it deserves. While this arrangement would call for some special agreement between PAHO's Emergency Preparedness and Relief Office and WHO's Emergency Relief Operations Office regarding the direction of the disaster preparedness activities in the Americas, the other regional offices of WHO are hardly in a position to institute similar offices.

While it is important to establish disaster preparedness programs in disaster-prone developing countries, the WHO could also institute relief preparedness activities for its own personnel. There are a number of possibilities for expansion into this area. For example, some briefings in an introductory way are given to WHO personnel preparing for field assignments. This is normally done at headquarters as part of an official's overall orientation to WHO's administrative procedures. However, a much wider scope of information could be disseminated and a program of continuing in-service training could be initiated and administered by the regional offices. This program could focus on two general aspects of personnel training:

1) <u>Disaster awareness education</u>. Many, if not most, WHO personnel have had little disaster experience. At the very least, the Office of Emergency Relief Operations could undertake steps to ensure that country representatives are sensitized to the problems of emergency health care and to the vulnerability of a particular population. Skills in transferring this awareness to ministers of health in disaster-prone developing countries should also be discussed and developed.

2) <u>Managerial training</u>. Relief programs are doomed to failure if administrative and operational aspects are poorly managed. In the past, relief efforts have been more seriously impaired by the lack of proper management than by the neglect or ignorance of nutritional principles or techniques.

In crisis situation it is important to make sure that field representatives are fully aware of the administrative procedures involved in communication with headquarters, assessing the disaster situation, formulating requests and managing the receipt and handling of medical supplies. There have been some problems in the past with dual reporting lines - one to the regional office and one to headquarters. This duplication and the delay that results might be somewhat alleviated if a WHO liaison officer were appointed or at least this function assigned during times of disaster. This officer could be someone who serves on a rotating basis from headquarters or the regional office, or part of the field staff, who would report directly to headquarters and serve as a liaison officer with the regional office.(34) An alternative to this suggestion would be to delegate responsibility for technical assessment and coordination at the local level to the regional offices of WHO.

In order to implement these suggestions regarding the education and training of World Health Organization officials dealing with disasters, a program of orientation and in-service training should be designed and administered by the Emergency Relief Operations Office. One of the major problems in implementing this suggestion is the lack of adequate funding for extensive training and refresher courses for WHO officials in disaster management.   Another problem is the lack of adequate training material and documents on proper disaster health management.   However, PAHO is presently considering the preparation of training material and courses on management.   Subject to the availability of extra-budgetary funds, this training will take place at the end of 1978 or in early 1979.

In 1975, WHO initiated a management survey at the headquarters levels of the Emergency Relief Operations Office to study the interrelationships between this office and various organization entities both within and without WHO, so far as they were related to disaster relief.(35)   One of the recommendations made by the 1975 management survey involving financial resources would seem to support an expansion in the use of the disaster account.

> Subject to the criteria and ceilings to be set by the Director-General, the administration of the "disaster account" of the Voluntary Fund for Health Promotion should be entrusted to the Responsible Officer of the Disaster Relief Office who should make efforts for the promotion of the fund and be held accountable for the records of its expenditure.(36)

Preparedness activities concerning the health sector of United Nations disaster relief operations might be promoted by setting aside a portion of the Voluntary Fund for Health Promotion for disaster preparedness and by appealing to member states to contribute to this disaster preparedness subaccount.

Another recommendation of the 1975 management survey stated the need for clarification of the functions of the Emergency Relief Operations Office and its relationships with the technical units and divisions at WHO headquarters.   The report cited difficulties in getting prompt information on proposed medical supplies for relief from the technical units. Besides a clarification of the disaster relief function, a stronger working arrangement might be established if there were some routine functional relationships with the technical units that were associated with disaster preparedness.   This has occurred to a limited extent with the training of paramedics and in the establishment of the basic drug list.   If the Emergency Relief Operations Office could become more involved in promoting and coordinating disaster preparedness programs, then an ongoing, noncrisis relationship could be maintained which could only benefit the interorganizational relationship during a relief operation.

Summary

   The primary purpose of a disaster preparedness program within WHO would be to specify and clarify responsibilities and relationships within the organization and to develop the managerial skills needed to administer timely and effective relief operations.
   The following suggestions are made as recommendations for promotion of disaster preparedness within the World Health Organization:

1) The promotion of emergency health care preparedness in disaster-prone developing countries should become a major priority for the World Health Organization.

2) The Emergency Relief Operations Office at the World Health Organization headquarters should be responsible for directing and coordinating disaster preparedness programs and for ensuring that emergency health care preparedness receives the high priority it deserves.

3) An agreement should be made between WHO/Geneva and the regional offices regarding the delays produced during a disaster relief operation through the technical validation of data. (See Fig. 2.1.)

4) Relief preparedness activities should become an integral part of any WHO personnel orientation, and such briefings should be conducted by the WHO Emergency Relief Operations Office.

5) In-service training programs should focus on the special problem of managing emergency health care operations, methods of nutritional surveillance and disaster preparedness programs.

6) The responsibilities of field offices, regional offices, and headquarters should be clarified and defined with regard to relief operations and disaster preparedness programs.

7) A WHO liaison officer should be appointed or assigned during times of disaster to report directly to headquarters and to be a liaison between the field office and the regional office. This officer could be someone who serves on a rotating basis from headquarters of the regional office or could be a field staff member.

8) The Director-General should expand the criteria for the use of the Voluntary Fund for Health Promotion monies to include a comprehensive program of disaster preparedness.

9)   Subject to the ceilings and criteria set by the
       Director-General, the administration of the
       Special Account for Disaster and Natural
       Catastrophes should be entrusted to the Re-
       sponsible Officer of the Emergency Relief
       Operation Office.(38)

10)   A subaccount for disaster preparedness should
       be established as part of the Voluntary Fund
       for Health Promotion. Promotion of this sub-
       account and expenditures should be entrusted
       to the Responsible Officer of the Emergency
       Relief Operation Office. A similar strategy is
       recommended for the use of PAHO's National
       Disaster Relief Voluntary Fund or the estab-
       lishment of a separate fund for disaster pre-
       paredness to enable additional resources to be
       directed to this activity.

While the occurrence of a disaster in a developing country
often causes a tragic loss of life and property, disaster preparedness can turn this tragedy into a positive force for
future development. Disaster preparedness can be considered
an opportunity to get rid of obstacles to effective emergency
health care and to promote new attitudes regarding the organization of such services. The World Health Organization
can, and should, play an active role in promoting this cause.

OFFICE OF THE UNITED NATIONS DISASTER
RELIEF COORDINATOR (UNDRO)

Relief Coordination

The Office of the United Nations Disaster Relief Coordinator was established in December 1971, by United Nations
General Assembly Resolution 2816 (XXVI). UNDRO is to
provide "an adequate permanent office in the United Nations
which shall be the focal point in the United Nations system for
disaster relief matters." Resolution 2816 provides for coordinating disaster relief and assisting governments in disaster
preparedness and prevention. UNDRO's mandate includes the
following:

1)   To mobilize, direct and co-ordinate the relief
       activities of the various organizations of the
       United Nations system in response to a request
       for disaster assistance from a stricken State;

2)   To co-ordinate United Nations assistance with
       assistance given by intergovernmental and

> non-governmental organizations, in particular
> by the International Red Cross;
3) To assist the Government of the stricken
country to assess its relief and other needs
and to evaluate the priority of those needs to
disseminate that information to prospective
donors and others concerned, and to serve as
a clearinghouse for assistance extended or
planned by all sources of external aid.(39)

Between March 1972 and March 1977, UNDRO was involved in
channeling almost $28 million for disaster relief in 94 disasters
in 60 different countries.(40) The operation of the United
Nations disaster relief system with UNDRO as focal point is
described in Chapter 2.

The staff of UNDRO was initially composed of the Disaster
Relief Coordinator (at the rank of Under-Secretary-General),
the director of the Office (a D-2), one professional officer
(P-5) and two General Service secretaries. In the following
two years, UNDRO was able to obtain additional staff, some of
whom had extensive relief background. Although UNDRO
needed more funds to improve its capabilities, it became very
difficult to persuade the General Assembly's Fifth Committee
and the Advisory Commitee on Administrative and Budgetary
Question (ACABO).(41)

In the beginning, UNDRO controlled no resources of its
own. A $200,000 account from the Working Capital Fund was
placed at the disposal of the Secretary-General by the General
Assembly. Allocations from the Working Capital Fund between
March 1972 and December 1973 amounted to $375,000.(42) The
move to strengthen the coordinating capacity of UNDRO began
in 1974 in response to the concern expressed in the
Secretary-General's report:

> ...while some progress has been made in the
> Office of the Disaster Relief Co-ordinator in es-
> tablishing its assigned function of mobilizing and
> co-ordinating relief, the lack of staff and facilities,
> combined with the frequency, duration and simul-
> taneity of disaster situations, has seriously impaired
> the effectiveness of the Office in discharging these
> and other responsibilities.(43)

The General Assembly responded to this concern of the
Secretary-General by calling for the strengthening of the
coordinating capacity of the office and authorizing a Voluntary
Fund for that purpose.(44) In addition to the establishment of
this fund, the coordinator had at his disposal $200,000 for the
biennium 1974-75, of which not more than $20,000 would be
allocated for any single disaster.

In 1975, the General Assembly acted again to strengthen UNDRO's coordination capacity and authorized two subaccounts within the Voluntary Fund established by Resolution 3243 (XXIX) and again in 1976 by Resolution 3440 (XXX). One subaccount was designed to enable UNDRO "to provide instantly emergency assistance." The purpose of this account was to enable the coordinator to increase the amount of assistance given for each disaster from $20,000 to $30,000. The second subaccount was designed

> ...to provide as an interim measure and pending review at a future date of alternative sources of financing, including the United Nations Development Programme, technical assistance to Governments for the elaboration of national plans for natural disaster prevention and preparedness. (45)

A target of $600,000 was established for program costs of technical assistance in disaster prevention and pre-disaster planning.

As a result of the General Assembly's 1974 resolution, and later minor changes, the number of posts was increased from the 15 provided for in the regular budget to 49. The additional staff was to be distributed between relief coordination and the pre-disaster planning and prevention division with a distribution of resources of 60 percent for coodination, 30 percent for disaster preparedness and 10 percent for prevention.

By the biennium 1976-77, the Working Capital Fund had proved to be an insufficient method of financing. It had been hoped that, by 1978, relief assistance would be fully financed from voluntary contributions. However, by September 30, 1977, only one contribution of $2,200 had been received in the emergency assistance subaccount toward the target figure of $400,000 for the biennium 1976-77. Therefore, it was necessary to retain regular budget allocation for a further two-year period from January 1, 1978, although the subaccount remained open for contributions. The financing of emergency assistance for 1978-79 will continue under the present mixed system of regular budget and voluntary contributions.

Since 1971, the coordination of international disaster relief operations has improved considerably, largely due to efforts to systematize the relationships between different participants in the United Nations disaster relief system. UNDRO has entered into formal arrangements with most of the United Nations agencies, which are either involved in disaster relief directly, or which have a special competence in activities related to disasters. (46) The purpose of these agreements is to regularize the United Nations relief response and provide greater uniformity to the system's relief efforts. The agree-

ments define the respective areas of competence of the coordination and the cooperating organizations and the aspects
of relief in which each will contribute. Despite these improvements in disaster relief coordination, there is much that
still needs to be done with regard to pre-disaster planning.

Disaster Preparedness and Prevention

In the pre-disaster phase, UNDRO was authorized:

a)   To promote the study, prevention, control and
      prediction of natural disasters, including the
      collection and dissemination of information
      concerning technological developments;
b)   To assist in providing advice to Governments
      on pre-disaster planning in association with
      relevant voluntary organizations, particularly
      with the League of Red Cross Societies, and to
      draw upon United Nations resources available
      for such purposes.(47)

A combination of factors has turned disaster relief coordination into a priority for UNDRO, while disaster preparedness and prevention have been severely limited. One of
the most important of these constraints was lack of funds. In
1973, UNDRO had at its disposal $25,000 to assist governments
in the elaboration of national preparations to meet natural
disasters. Supplemented by a $3,750 gift from a member
state, this sum of $28,750 comprised the entire disaster pre-
paredness and prevention budget.(48) Under the terms of
Resolution 3152, the Secretary-General was authorized, as an
interim measure, to draw upon the Working Capital Fund of
$45,000 in 1974 and $60,000 in 1975 for disaster preparedness
and prevention.(49)
In 1975, the ability of UNDRO to promote disaster prevention and preparedness programs was measurably enhanced
with the establishment of the technical assistance subaccount.(50) The subaccount for technical assistance to governments in disaster preparedness and prevention by September 30, 1977, had received $493,877 of its $600,000 targeted
figure. The governments of Japan, the United Kingdom and
the Netherlands have financed special projects outside the
subaccount.
During the biennium 1976-77, $412,200 was spent on
disaster preparedness and prevention, demonstrating an increased interest on the part of member states in these types of
programs, and an increased capability on the part of UNDRO
to meet such requests for assistance.
The Secretary-General identified in 1974 what should

comprise a United Nations strategy for preparedness and prevention. In that report it was proposed that:

> A decision by the international community to adopt a concerted international strategy would involve technical surveys and studies, the identification of specific projects in individual developing countries and the allocation of a proportion of funds normally earmarked for development purposes.(51)

UNDRO's general approach to disaster prevention has been to conduct technical studies in the state of the art, to prepare guidelines for development planning for areas vulnerable to disasters, and to collaborate with other agencies in joint research projects.

UNESCO and UNDRO have established an international committee known as the International Committee on Earthquake Risk. The new body was called for in a resolution adopted by the UNESCO Intergovernmental Conference on the Assessment and Mitigation of Earthquake Risk held in Paris in 1976. The purpose of the committee is to provide advice regarding the implementation of recommendations and resolutions of the conference and on the preparation of a long-term interdisciplinary research program, to be undertaken jointly by UNESCO and UNDRO.(52)

UNDRO has also started to explore with UNEP, ITU and COPUOS (Committee on the Peaceful Uses of Outer Space) the possibility of the use of a space technology capable of monitoring natural phenomena causing disasters. Possibilities exist for the coordinated establishment in the future of a system which could help monitor, predict and warn of natural disasters with the assistance of WMO systems.(53)

UNEP and UNDRO are closely cooperating on projects concerning disaster prevention and mitigation. Natural disasters have been designated a priority program area by UNEP, which adopted a resolution at the Fourth Session of the Governing Council requesting the Executive Director to accelerate program activities relating to natural disasters. UNEP has financially supported the World Survey of Disaster Damage and the overview of natural disasters, and is supporting the monographs on the state of existing knowledge in disaster prevention and mitigation.

A research project on emergency shelter and the provision of housing and related facilities was begun in 1976. The objective of the project is to assist vulnerable countries in contingency plans for the most effective ways of providing accommodation for disaster victims. Its first phase has been completed.

In 1975, UNDRO began a World Survey of Disaster Damage for the period 1960-1974. This study aims at providing the international community with some of the data needed for the formulation of an international disaster prevention strategy. UNDRO has also been studying the state of the art in disaster prevention and mitigation. Five chapters of the study have been completed which deal with the seismological, vulcanological, hydrological, meteorological and land-use aspects of disaster prevention. The eight remaining chapters planned include those on engineering, health, community preparedness, public information, economic, sociological, legal and vulnerability analysis.(54)

Three manuals on the implications of disasters for the planning, building, and management of human settlements were completed in 1976. These guidelines are written in non-technical language and are designed for government officials and community leaders, who are called upon to approve projects which may be in areas of high risk.(55)

The first Disaster Preparedness and Relief Seminar in the South Pacific region was held in Suva, Fiji from September 20 to 26, 1976. The seminar was organized by the League of Red Cross Societies with the support of UNDRO, in cooperation with the government of Fiji and the Commonwealth Secretariat. Following one of the seminar's recommendations, plans are now being considered by UNDRO, the League of Red Cross Societies and the South Pacific Bureau for Economic Cooperation (SPEC) to hold a regional workshop on regional disaster relief and preparedness.

Joint UNDRO/UNDP meetings on disaster prevention, preparedness and relief coordination have been held for the Resident Representatives of disaster-prone countries in Europe, the Mediterranean, the Middle East, Asia and Pacific and Latin American regions. The purpose of the meetings was to give further orientation to Resident Representatives in their duties relating to relief coordination, and to discuss the importance of host government and donor preparedness, the role of prevention and the impact of disaster on development.

Between April 1972 and April 1977, UNDRO provided experts to 18 different countries to give advice about the writing of national disaster plans (see Appendix C). The missions provided advice on administration and management, stockpiling of supplies and earmarking of funds, preparation of national, regional and local plans and training for local personnel. Only nine of the countries receiving UNDRO assistance are on the list of LDC/MSA countries (see Table 3.1). This is noteworthy because 80 percent of these countries have received international disaster relief assistance since 1972. Some of these nine countries who have had UNDRO's technical assistance still do not have a national disaster organization or national disaster plan. Beyond the technical missions and provisions of experts, UNDRO has not yet provided substantial assistance to governments to enable them to act upon the advice and recommendations proposed by the missions.

UNDRO has experienced an increase in requests for these advisory missions, but has not been able to meet all of them. The increasing interest on the part of disaster-prone developing countries indicates that the United Nations must find a way to supplement its present disaster preparedness activities by developing a new comprehensive approach to the subject.

Resolution 2816 (XXVI), which established UNDRO, invites disaster-prone governments

    a)   To establish disaster contingency plans with appropriate assistance from the Disaster Relief Co-ordinator;

    b)   To appoint a single national disaster relief co-ordinator to facilitate the receipt of international aid in times of emergency;

    c)   To establish stockpiles of emergency supplies, such as tents, blankets, medicines and non-perishable foodstuffs;

    d)   To make necessary arrangements for the training of administrative and relief personnel;

    e)   To consider appropriate legislative or other measures to facilitate the receipt of aid, including overflight rights and the necessary privileges and immunities for relief units; and

    f)   To improve national disaster warning systems.(56)

In response to this concern, a number of proposals were prepared by UNDRO and LORCS in 1977 to expedite international relief. The following recommendations were made to disaster-prone governments to improve their programs of disaster preparedness, thereby expediting disaster relief operations:

    1)   Establishment of a single national relief authority to coordinate all domestic relief activities and to collaborate with the appropriate government departments and domestic and international relief agencies;

    2)   Waiver of requirements for consular invoices and certificates of origin with respect to relief consignments, on condition that adequate documentation from recognized relief agencies accompany such consignments;

    3)   Waiver of requirements for import and/or export licenses for relief shipments destined for any kind of disaster;

    4)   Waiver of normal requirements regarding fumigation certificates and restrictions on food imports where these would impede the admission of relief items;

5) Waiver of requirements for transit, entry and
    exit visas for relief personnel;
6) Restriction of relief contributions to the high-
    priority needs identified by the appropriate
    relief authorities and agencies;
7) Institution of educational programs for donors
    on the importance of avoiding contributions of
    nonessential relief items;
8) Prompt notification to consignees of impending
    relief shipments, review of consignment
    procedures and report on the arrival of con-
    signments by the consignee;
9) Ensurance of standing instructions to expedite
    processing of relief shipments;
10) Authorization of national airlines to accord
    free transportation at minimal rates for relief
    consignments and relief personnel;
11) Relaxation of limitations on carriers not pos-
    sessing traffic rights;
12) Accordance of overflight permission and land-
    ing rights for aircraft transporting inter-
    national relief at the outset of disaster emer-
    gency operations; and
13) Authorization of relief agency personnel to
    have access to all available communication
    facilities. (57)

These recommendations provide guidelines for diaster-prone
countries in designing their own disaster preparedness
strategies.
    The creation of the subaccount for diaster preparedness
and prevention was always to be regarded as an interim
measure pending review at a future date of alternative sources
of funding. General Assembly Resolution 3152 requested the
Secretary-General to explore various means to implement disaster preparedness and prevention programs, including
support from UNDP.(58) At that time (1973), conversations
with UNDP revealed that UNDP resources for many of the
country programs for the current five-year planning period
were fully committed, with the result that the inclusion of
pre-disaster planning activities in UNDP country programs was
not likely in the immediate future.

    Other possible means of support will continue to be
    explored, but it seems clear that broader action is
    necessary if, in the long run, the destructive
    impact of disasters on the economies of developing
    countries are to be prevented or reduced.(59)

In 1976, UNDRO was again faced with a problem in integrating its technical assistance programs with UNDP. Two regional projects in disaster prevention, for which UNDRO hoped to receive assistance from UNDP funds, were postponed but a preliminary mission connected with one of the regional projects has taken place.(60)

Given the present mandate of UNDRO, it is unrealistic to expect the office to perform beyond its capabilities in the field of disaster preparedness and prevention. In assessing the performance of UNDRO in disaster relief, it is important to remember that the office has not been in existence very long, it has ‘had substantial problems in financing, and it was not intended to be an operational organization. However, given the present mandate there are a number of things UNDRO could do to increase its effectiveness in the field of disaster preparedness:

1) A clearer definition of the precise nature of UNDRO's advisory services should be made, keeping in mind that UNDRO has neither the resource capability or mandate to be operationally active in the field.

2) UNDRO should identify and articulate a United Nations system-wide strategy of disaster preparedness.

3) UNDRO should encourage the increasing involvement of United Nations organizations in their own programs of disaster preparedness.

4) UNDRO should work out arrangements with the other United Nations organizations involved in disaster preparedness regarding their respective responsibilities and relationships.

5) A greater effort should be made to promote in-service disaster training of United Nations field personnel.

6) UNDRO should give priority to the training of disaster relief administrators at the national, district and local levels in disaster-prone developing countries.

7) Those least developed countries and most seriously affected should be targeted for special assistance as those areas most vulnerable to natural disasters.

8) A concerted effort should be made to employ the services of the most qualified and experienced disaster preparedness experts available for technical advisory mission.

The Office of the United Nations Disaster Relief Coordinator has been the focal point for United Nations disaster

relief assistance as well as disaster preparedness and prevention since March 1972. The effect of this mandate in the
field of preparedness has thus been to dissuade other United
Nations development agencies from undertaking separate disaster preparedness activities.

One cannot discuss the operation of UNDRO or the role of
the United Nations system in disaster without discussing the
vital role of the United Nations Development Programme Resident Representatives. Besides the fact that these representatives have a critical role in disaster relief operations, UNDP
also has an important function in disaster preparedness
programming.

THE UNITED NATIONS DEVELOPMENT PROGRAMME (UNDP)

General Assembly Resolution 2816 (XXVI) takes note of
"the key role which the Resident Representatives of the United
Nations Development Programme could play at the country
level...."(61) The role of UNDP with regard to disasters
actually falls into three general categories: relief, reconstruction and disaster planning and preparedness. Because of
the importance of the Resident Representative as the representative of the United Nations in developing countries, UNDP
can and should play a vital role in disaster preparedness
activities.

The communications and reporting aspect of UNDP's role
in disaster relief coordination has already been discussed in
Chapter 2. Apart from the Resident Representative's role as
UNDRO's "arm in the field," there are other provisions for
independent relief activity. Resident Representatives may
request up to $20,000 from UNDP for disaster emergencies.
Further, there are provisions for utilizing their imprest
account for immediate purchases for a specific amount and for
the items agreed upon (authorized by the UNDP Division of
Finance). Only UNDRO's contribution is reimbursed to UNDP.

UNDRO has instructed the Resident Representatives to
create an ad hoc task force, which is comprised of representatives of the United Nations and other relevant agencies in
the area. It has been recommended that this task force be
established permanently as a standing United Nations Disaster
Team. The purpose of this team would be to define roles and
elaborate details of cooperation for disaster emergencies, and
identify personnel, supplies and vehicles which, in critical
situations, could be temporarily diverted to the needs of
disaster relief.(62)

Ideally, the United Nations Disaster Team would hold
regular meetings and establish a permanent liaison with the
government disaster coordinator. An effort should be made to
invite to these meetings representatives of foreign embassies,

which traditionally offer disaster relief, and local and international voluntary agencies. Experiences with these teams in
disaster situations have varied considerably, but it is a good
management concept, and has, in general, worked well.

In the area of rehabilitation and reconstruction, General
Assembly Resolution 2816 (XXVI), paragraph 1(i) requires the
Disaster Relief Coordinator:

> To phase out relief operations under his aegis as
> the stricken country moves into the stage of re-
> habilitation and reconstruction, but to continue to
> interest himself, within the framework of his re-
> sponsibilities for relief, in the activities of the
> United Nations agencies concerned with re-
> habilitation and reconstruction.

The Resident Representative can play a useful role in
disaster-prone developing countries by contributing to
bringing about an awareness of the risks involved and of what
can be done to reduce them. In this respect, the rehabilitation and reconstruction activities of UNDP can be very important. After a disaster specific measures can be taken to
avoid the recurrence of past mistakes.

In addition to emergency disaster relief (up to $20,000),
UNDP has authority to provide funds from its program reserve
for projects related to rehabilitation, especially rehabilitation
planning. In the event of a disaster, Resident Representatives
may take the initiative in discussing with the governments
concerned the need for any UNDP program reserve resources
for projects involving rehabilitation. The Regional Bureau is
then consulted regarding the project specifications.

The Resident Representative's main role with respect to
disaster prevention and preparedness lies in his or her
capacity to be the focal point for the formulation of the country programs for UNDP technical cooperation. The Representative should serve as a catalyst to promote awareness of
certain problems and should stimulate action taken by the
government. The Resident Representative is in a unique
position to perform this task. Already in the country and
familiar with local conditions, the Representative should be
able to impress upon the government the importance of disaster
preparedness and assist in these planning and training
arrangements.

In November 1972, UNDRO issued a set of guidelines to
Resident Representatives detailing their responsibilities when
disaster strikes and requesting that they play a vital role with
respect to pre-disaster planning and preparedness. These
guidelines concentrated primarily on the relief activities of the
Resident Representatives, but in August 1975, a revised set of
instructions included information about responsibilities in the

field of preparedness and prevention.(63) These guidelines
suggest that government authorities should be sensitized to
three factors when planning country programs of technical
cooperation: 1) natural disasters have a severe impact on
development; 2) most forms of natural disasters (as distinct
from the natural phenomena which cause them) can be prevented or at least mitigated; and 3) some of the most basic
and effective preventive measures are also among the least
costly.

Resident Representatives have been instrumental in
setting up permanent disaster relief focal points for dealing
with disasters and making disaster plans. UNDP is also
financing specific projects designed, if not precisely to an-
ticipate disasters, at least to offset their consequences.(64)

UNDRO has requested detailed information from the
Resident Representatives on the present status of disaster
preparedness in their respective countries. This request has
not produced the quantity or quality of information desired.
Part of the problem may be a lack of awareness or lack of time
and staff to compile such information. Another more basic
reason is that in many countries such information is non-
existent or not available. Based on this information, the
guidelines given to the Resident Representatives suggest that
a strategy for action be defined at the country level according
to the risks involved and other pertinent factors. In countries which are particularly disaster-prone, this may include
recommendations for inclusion in the country programs of
projects focusing on disaster preparedness and prevention.

UNDP country programs offer a unique opportunity to
integrate disaster preparedness and prevention within the
development planning process. For example, in Mauritius
UNDP and WMO have collaborated on a meteorlgical training
project. In Madagascar, both organizations are helping to
establish a cyclone and thunderstorm forecasting, detection
and warning system. In 1975, a joint UNDP/UNDRO/ECLA
mission studied the possibility of minimizing the damage caused
by natural disasters in Central America. One result of this
study has been the creation of a small-scale project, financed
by UNDP. The objectives of this project are to: 1) develop a
methodology for the analysis of vulnerability to natural disasters; 2) integrate this into the methodology process of
economic, social and physical planning; 3) formulate and
execute investment projects and recommend a suitable international framework.(65)

Disaster prevention is not necessarily an additional
element of development, but it is an aspect of it. This is an
important distinction, for in many years, the inclusion of
disaster prevention aspects in country programs does not
always constitute an additional cost factor.

There are a number of other ways in which Resident

Representatives could facilitate the implementation of disaster preparedness programs at the country level. A concerted effort on the part of the UNDP field offices may require more staff, time and resources than are currently available. In addition, the Resident Represenatives already have so many responsibilities as the focal point for the United Nations in a country, that the responsibility of yet another task may be too much to ask. Therefore, an effort should be made to provide administrative support for carrying out the disaster preparedness responsibilities of the UNDP field office.

One suggestion for dividing the responsibility and the labor involved in carrying out these activities might be to expand the use of the United Nations Disaster Team. The standing United Nations Disaster Team is intended to facilitate the task of the Resident Representative in arriving at an accurate assessment of the international aid required. In this sense, the United Nations Disaster Team is serving not only a relief coordination function, but a disaster preparedness function as well. The preparedness activities, however, are confined to United Nations and do not extend to the preparedness of the disaster-prone regions.

While disaster preparedness programs should be coordinated with long-term development assistance, special emphasis should be given to preparedness so that it receives sufficient attention and does not have to compete with longer-term objectives. At the present time, disaster preparedness, as a separate kind of development programming exercise, does not exist within UNDP. While certain aspects of preparedness are found within long-term development assistance, there is no special focus upon this aspect of development. Resident Representatives should be in a position to inform governments of the available resources for disaster preparedness, much in the same way that they advise disaster-stricken governments about relief assistance available through the United Nations system and, in nondisaster situations, about development assistance available. With the exception of UNDRO's technical advisory missions, at the present time there is no place within the United Nations to fund a disaster preparedness project.

In order to remove disaster preparedness from the competition for development funds, different alternatives have been discussed. One of these ideas involves increasing UNDRO's disaster preparedness budget. Another idea which has been discussed involves the establishment of a trust fund for disaster preparedness. This fund would be administered by UNDP and would rely entirely on voluntary contributions. The fund would be created for the purpose of financing specific projects of disaster preparedness in developing countries. This financing would be for projects not now covered by the medium and long-term development programs. UNDRO would be the executing agency responsible for project determination, selection of experts, etc.

A number of proposals are suggested for increased UNDP involvement in disaster preparedness:

1) The United Nations Development Programme should identify disaster preparedness as a special priority area for increased focus in development planning.

2) The Resident Representative should provide the in-country focal point for the United Nations Programme for Disaster Preparedness with administrative support from UNDP headquarters and/or UNDRO.

3) The Resident Pepresentative should play an active part in preparing the United Nations Disaster Team for more efficient disaster relief operations.

4) The Resident Representative should continue to bring to the attention of government officials in disaster-prone countries the need for greater disaster preparedness measures.

5) The Resident Representative should assist UNDRO in advising governments of the international assistance available for implementing operational programs of disaster preparedness.

6) In this regard, a trust fund for disaster preparedness projects should be created and administered by UNDP and financed by voluntary contributions for realizing such proposed programs.

7) UNDP should make a concerted effort to integrate disaster preparedness projects within the medium- and longer-term development programs in the least developed countries.

8) Assignment to disaster-prone countries poses very great responsibilities and should be taken into account in headquarters' selection of Resident Representatives and their staff.

9) In-service training in disaster relief should be instituted in order to strengthen the field offices and better prepare those personnel already in disaster-prone areas with the necessary skills to handle relief operations.

10) The scope of the United Nations Disaster Team should be expanded to provide the administrative support for promoting and administering disaster preparedness measures.

From the preceding discussion, it appears that most of the United Nations activities in the area of natural disasters is confined to relief operations. The present state of preparedness within the United Nations organizations, and the present state of their efforts to promote a strategy for disaster preparedness in the developing world is far from from being satisfactory. There are a great number of deficiencies in the United Nations approach which require accelerated efforts for implementation.

One serious deficiency in the United Nations disaster relief system that has been revealed in past practice is the absence of program-support funds for disaster preparedness in developing countries that are demonstrably disaster-prone. This problem was most strikingly illustrated during the Sahelian and Ethiopian drought disasters, and a shortage of logistical equipment and trained personnel has remained a critical problem in many subsequent relief operations.

One way to approach the problem of the shortage of trained personnel is to make better use of the valuable human resources available in the disaster-stricken country. In many disasters, most of the rescue and relief operations are done by neighbors, and in many instances, these neighbors are part of a local organization or cooperative. In Guatemala, following the earthquake in 1976, a considerable distribution of relief supplies, housing materials, and organization of labor - even the administrative accounting for the relief materials - was accomplished through a network of cooperatives. While cooperatives are not usually thought of as playing a major role in disaster relief, or even in disaster preparedness, they are very often an important factor in mobilizing the public to take preventive action against the threat of disasters.

The principle of popular participation in development activities has long been recognized. The report of the United Nations Economic and Social Council on the objectives of the Second United Nations Development Decade (April 1970) stated that:

> Popular participation in development, to be effective, must be so organized as to minimize the weakness inherent in smallness of scale and to maximize the benefits that can be derived from group action; the co-operation formula is eminently suited for this purpose. Its contribution is not, however, limited to spheres of production, consumption and income distribution.(66)

The principle of popular participation is also important for the success of any disaster relief operation and any successful disaster preparedness program. The emergence of many types of cooperative movements throughout the developing world illustrates the flexibility of this type of organization as an instrument of economic and social progress. Because of the importance of cooperatives in national development, and there-

fore in disaster relief and preparedness, it is important at this
point to examine in more detail how the United Nations can
promote disaster preparedness through already established
institutions in disaster-prone developing countries. The
following discussion will describe the activities of the International Labour Organisation (ILO) and how the cooperative
model can be used to institute disaster preparedness programs.

THE ILO, COOPERATIVES, AND DISASTER PREPAREDNESS

The International Labour Organisation (ILO) has been
concerned, since its inception, with the promotion of cooperatives. Aid in the cooperative field, principally for developing countries, is among the oldest and most widespread of
ILO's technical assistance programs. This tradition has
recently been supplemented by disaster-related activities.

Disasters and the ILO

In 1974, when a cyclone hit Honduras, the ILO already
had two teams of experts there - one for vocational training
and guidance and the other for employment. The work
programs of both teams and projects were immediately adapted
to the disaster circumstances. With extra support from UNDP,
ILO reorganized its priorities. In 1976, when Guatemala suffered a serious earthquake, ILO took part in an interagency
mission to assess the recovery needs of the area. A UNDP-
financed project for employment planning and national reconstruction was later administered by ILO.

In 1977, a memorandum of understanding was signed
specifying the relationship between the ILO and UNDRO.
According to this agreement,

> UNDRO activities concern three main areas, namely
> disaster prevention, disaster preparedness and
> disaster relief co-ordination; the ILO will co-operate
> with UNDRO in these three areas, in all those fields
> which fall within its technical competence.(67)

The ILO can give advice and technical assistance for the
prevention of natural disasters and for reconstruction after a
disaster. The ILO and UNDRO cooperate in organizing labor-
intensive work programs for disaster prevention and in assessing needs for employment, training and rehabilitation.
Such activities include vocational training (particularly for
construction, transport, civil engineering and public works),

vocational rehabilitation of the disabled, and development of the managerial abilities of small-scale industrialists and leaders of cooperatives.

This kind of involvement is very important because a sudden disaster may cause large numbers of people to be temporarily out of work, and this requires some sort of emergency employment scheme. The need to formulate and implement programs at very short notice can put considerable strain on the administrative and design capacity of the government officials. It is necessary to divert government staff from their normal duties to assist in running an emergency program. These considerations influence the type of projects that are selected. Emergency assistance work projects may be brought in that have little relevance to the overall development plan of the regions concerned.

One suggestion that has been made to alleviate these post-disaster problems concerns disaster preparedness. A "pipeline" of emergency projects has been proposed which would prepare government officials for emergency employment following a sudden disaster. Building up a stockpile of readily designed projects ready to be implemented, and which could be put into operation at short notice, would help to alleviate some of the strain on governmental administrative and design capacity.

The concept of a pipeline is not the same as a "shelf of reserve projects," which usually have low priority and may have no relevance to the economic growth objectives of the affected region. The pipeline concept is a system of organizing public works planning so that programs, for a number of years, are simultaneously in the process of preparation with standard designs and varying degrees of completeness. Within a long-term period, there is a constant revolving process of new projects as they pass from the design stage to the beginning of operations. In the event of a sudden disaster, the local authorities of the affected region can readily draw upon this pipeline.(68)

Another possibility for ILO involvement in disaster preparedness concerns an area in which ILO has long experience and expertise - cooperative development. Disaster preparedness through cooperatives is a good strategy for the following reasons:

1) Cooperatives can provide an institution with a membership, a structure and internal organization in areas lacking institutional frameworks.

2) Cooperatives are recognized by governments and others in developing countries as appropriate and flexible instruments for national development.

3) Since cooperatives are based on self-help and initiative, local leadership is essential. Local initiative is also essential for the success of disaster preparedness.

4) Cooperatives can help in generating employment opportunities, and therefore provide a link with the human resources available.

5) Cooperatives may provide technically qualified staff in skills relevant to disaster preparedness, or at least may provide the format for training and education.

Technical assistance in developing a strategy of disaster preparedness through cooperative institutions has to be based on clear policy commitments on the part of governments. In some countries, lip service is paid to the need for cooperatives, but the prerequisites for success (e.g., policy commitments, resources for development, adequate supervisory and technical government support) have not been provided.

Cooperatives that are already established are most often used at the local level to assist in disaster relief operations. Sometimes, however, cooperatives have been formed after a disaster for food distribution. This is a good opportunity to build beyond this newly formed structure and institute disaster preparedness as one of the purposes of the cooperative. It must be remembered, however, that there must be other reasons for forming the cooperative on a permanent basis, and future plans of employment and income must be built into the design from the beginning. Otherwise the cooperative will fold at the end of the food aid period, as happened in southern Tunisia following a relief operation.

In some countries where cooperatives are relatively well established and facilities and institutions available in several fields, the task of including disaster preparedness activities should be relatively easy. There may be countries in a region with common interests in cooperative development, which are unable to sponsor or absorb individually large-scale technical assistance because of their size or the limitation of national resources. Advisory services and disaster relief management training can be offered on a regional basis, especially in areas which have similar disaster hazards and socioeconomic conditions. An important product of such a regional approach can be an exchange of information about common disaster relief problems, and may lead to the establishment of a regional disaster preparedness strategy which could benefit all countries.

Activities of a disaster preparedness nature which could be promoted by the ILO include establishing a local disaster relief committee, organizing volunteer fire and rescue teams, organizing volunteer medical aides, youth groups, etc., training of volunteer rescue personnel in basic techniques necessary in disaster relief, education of the populace to disaster hazards and what they can do about them. Basically the ILO is in the business of mobilizing labor, and the participation of labor is the key to success for any disaster preparedness effort.

Summary

The ILO not only has an important role in giving advice and providing technical assistance after a disaster, but can also play an active part in pre-disaster planning as well. The ILO has at least two avenues through which to promote disaster preparedness activities:

    1)   Emergency employment schemes; and
    2)   Cooperatives.

Emergency employment as a type of disaster relief can be handled more effectively if contingency plans are made prior to the disaster event. The pipeline approach to emergency project planning seems to be most suitable for fulfilling this need. However, in order for this pipeline to benefit a country, one must wait for a disaster to occur before bringing forward these projects. Therefore, the ILO needs to take a more activist posture.

Disaster preparedness through established cooperatives is recommended as a method of introducing this type of development activity to disaster-prone developing countries. Cooperatives are recognized by governments as appropriate instruments for development and can provide the institutional support, local leadership and manpower resources to establish education and training programs related to disaster preparedness.

Cooperatives provide people with a way to become involved in their own development. By stimulating positive attitudes in the community and removing the tendency to become dependent on continuous government and international aid, the climate is ripe for disaster preparedness self-help programs. Disaster preparedness through cooperatives can be seen as a means of reducing the relief burdens on governments and international agencies. By employing these two methods, emergency employment planning and the wider use of cooperatives, disaster preparedness can be effectively integrated into the longer-term development program, and reduce the short-term costs of disaster relief as well.

The United Nations organizations have been instructed, through resolutions dealing with natural disaster, to assist disaster-stricken member states, and, through other resolutions, to give special assistance to combat the worst effects of poverty in the least developed and most severely affected

countries. Together these resolutions form a formidable commitment to poor disaster-prone countries. The commitment of
the United Nations and its activities in the area of natural
disaster relief has already been discussed. The relationship of
disasters to development and the commitment to assist the least
developed and most seriously affected countries have also been
examined. Recognizing the importance of these commitments
and the serious effect of natural disasters, as well as the
effects that other types of emergencies have had upon the
poorest in the developing world, a new approach has been
taken which further strengthens the need for disaster preparedness and the United Nations commitment to assist those in
need.

ECONOMIC EMERGENCY SITUATIONS

An earthquake or typhoon is always striking news and
will receive immediate attention, but this is not the case of the
permanent or semipermanent economic emergency situation of
the least developed and most seriously affected countries,
unless a sustained effort is made to monitor and improve
perceptions of its causes, remedies and implications. The case
of the Sahel region in Africa is an illustrative example. The
widespread drought and subsequent agricultural disaster which
caused famine in this region reached a particularly disastrous
point in 1973. Most of the countries in the region (Chad,
Mali, Mauritania, Niger, Senegal, and Upper Volta) were
visited by FAO experts and the famine was foreseen at least
two years before it happened. The massive international relief
effort, in most places, came too late - after thousands of
people had already died of starvation.
    At the same time that greater emphasis was being placed
upon a reorganization of the international disaster relief
system, there also emerged a concern over the apparent in-
adequacy of development programs in reaching those most in
need of assistance. Deliberations in the United Nations began
to call for a rethinking of development aid directed toward the
poorest of the poor, whose lives have been relatively un-
touched by previous development programs.
    Natural disasters in some of the poorest of those coun-
tries (e.g., Bangladesh, Ethiopia, Haiti, the Sahelian countries) revealed that there exists a state of permanent emergency in many regions of the world - areas in which even
relatively minor natural disasters produce massive repercussions. In 1975, the General Assembly, through Resolution
3510, requested that the Secretary-General submit proposals
regarding the means with which the United Nations system can
deal with economic emergency situations and meet the needs of
the affected populations.

The term "emergency" has usually been applied to situations arising from sudden major natural disasters, such as earthquakes and floods, that have "inflicted heavy loss of life and property" and to their "serious economic and social consequences for all especially the developing countries."(69) However, the view was expressed at the fifty-seventh session of the Economic and Social Council and the thirtieth and sixth special sessions of the General Assembly, that the concept of an emergency transcends the restrictive notion of disaster situations to encompass: 1) permanent or semipermanent emergency situations, and 2) disaster-like economic emergency situations brought about by economic crises and foreign aggression and occupation.(70)

A permanent or semipermanent emergency situation exists where the levels of living remain consistently far below international norms deemed necessary for a healthy and productive life. This category of emergency situations characterizes the living conditions of many of the LDC and MSA countries. Disaster-like economic emergency situations may be brought about by either natural disasters or political developments, but are characterized by economic crises. In accordance with General Assembly Resolution 2626 (XXV), the international community has a responsibility to assist these affected countries.(71) In response to resolution 3510 (XXX), the Secretary-General appointed an ad hoc task force to prepare a report on the implementation of this resolution. In a later report submitted by the Secretary-General to the Economic and Social Council in 1976, it was noted that the first two types of emergency situations - disasters and permanent or semipermanent emergencies - were being adequately dealt with by the existing United Nations arrangements. In the third type of situation - disaster-like economic emergencies - it was suggested that more systematic procedures might be established.(72)

At ECOSOC's sixty-third session, a number of criteria were proposed by the Secretary-General for identifying a disaster-like economic emergency situation.(73) In general, these criteria are designed to be flexible enough to permit immediate assistance when it is needed, as well as restrictive enough to differentiate disaster-like economic emergencies from disaster situations being dealt with by UNDRO and permanent or semipermanent situations being dealt with in other ways and other contexts. A further recommendation involved setting up new arrangements and procedures for assistance to countries suffering from disaster-like economic emergencies.

As a result of these discussions, the establishment of an intersecretariat unit has been proposed to coordinate the international community's response to these emergencies. This proposal would place the United Nations response to emergency situations which are not presently covered within UNDRO's mandate under the direct authority of the Secretary-General. The functions of this proposed unit are:

a) To assess data referred to it by the system indicating the possibility or probability of disaster-like economic emergencies and to recommend, where necessary, measures for preventive action by the system;

b) To act, in the event of a disaster-like economic emergency, as the system's focal point for receiving data concerning the nature of the emergency and the impact on the affected populations;

c) On the basis of all available information received and assessed, to make recommendations to the Secretary-General for co-ordinated practical measures to respond to the requests of Governments;

d) To assist the Secretary-General in co-ordinating the implementation of such measures and to monitor their results; and

e) After the occurrence of a natural disaster, at the point where the Office of the United Nations Disaster Relief Co-ordinator begins to phase out its humanitarian relief operations, to co-ordinate the system's participation in the follow-up of the rehabilitation and reconstruction activities. (74)

This machinery would be established on an interagency basis, but would not have any permanent membership. The unit would be a small one and would rely heavily upon the organizations of the United Nations system which have direct relevance to the specific emergency and upon the UNDP Resident Representatives to communicate the information necessary for the unit's functioning.

A government may wish the Secretary-General to make a formal proclamation of a disaster-like economic emergency. Presumably this announcement would aid in mobilizing assistance. However, it is more likely that government would not wish to make such an announcement. As in a natural disaster situation, governments should have the option of requesting assistance without declaring an emergency. This arrangement would be possible under the provisions of this unit.

No action was taken upon this proposal at the thirty-second session of the General Assembly and the position of the United Nations with regard to intervention in these cases is not very clear at the present time. If an arrangement is arrived at involving the Secretary-General's office, the lessons

learned from the experience already acquired in handling
natural disaster situations should be applied. It has been
suggested that following a natural disaster, at the point where
UNDRO begins to phase out its relief operations, this unit
might coordinate the United Nations system's participation in
the rehabilitation and reconstruction activities that follow.
There is a precedent for this type of action in the establishment of the United Nations Sahelian Office (UNSO) following
the drought disaster in that part of sub-Saharan Africa known
as the Sahel. The purpose of this unit was to identify
medium- and long-term development program strategies for the
area, and UNSO now coordinates international assistance for
specific projects proposed by the Comite Permanent Interetats
de Lutte contre la Secheresse dans le Sahel (CILSS). At the
rehabilitation and reconstruction phase, there might be a good
opportunity to integrate a strategy for disaster preparedness,
providing yet another way to introduce this aspect of planning
into the development programs of LDC and MSA countries.
     Other United Nations organizations have taken a number
of special measures to combat the effects of permanent or
semipermanent emergency situations. For example, UNDP has
allocated, in addition to the indicative planning figures, $45.5
million and granted local cost waivers to these countries.(75)
FAO has given priority to these countries in its technical
assistance programs. The World Bank and the International
Development Association (IDA) have expanded assistance to
these countries since 1975, and have devoted 38 percent of all
commitments to them. In the case of IDA, 84 percent or about
$1,256 million has been invested in the least developed
world.(76)
     The United Nations Conference on Trade and Development
(UNCTAD) has for some years been concerned with permanent
or semipermanent emergency situations. In resolution 98 (IV),
UNCTAD IV recommended special measures be taken in favor of
the least developed countries in the area of financial and
technical assistance. These measures include cancelling the
official debts of these countries, giving highly concessional
terms for the other outstanding debt burdens and giving
highly concessional loans.(77)
     With regard to disaster-like economic emergencies,
UNCTAD IV recommended that the appropriate organs of the
United Nations system give assistance to the Comoros because
of its serious and disturbing economic situation, with a further
recommendation that similar measures be taken in other newly
independent African states.(78) UNCTAD IV has also recommended assistance in the preparation of national and regional
plans for disaster preparedness, and the organization of relief
efforts and training and advisory services to be extended to
the least developed, developing islands and developing land-
locked countries.

In 1974, the Executive Board of UNICEF proclaimed a "Declaration of Emergency for Children in Developing Countries as a Result of the Recent Economic Crisis." The declaration authorized immediate special assistance to children in the least developed and most seriously affected countries. Whether a situation is classified as a permanent or semipermanent emergency or as a disaster-like economic emergency, the needs of children are essentially the same, requiring basically the same kind of response. UNICEF concentrates its regular assistance to these countries, and is also authorized to seek voluntary contributions for special assistance. Some $55 million was raised for this purpose in 1976 as compared with $34 million in 1975.(79)

The governing body of World Food Programme has defined emergencies as

> ...urgent situations in which there is clear evidence that an event has occurred which causes human suffering or loss of livestock and which the Government concerned has not the means to remedy; and it is a demonstrably abnormal event which produces dislocation in the life of the community on an exceptional scale.(80)

This definition covers: a) sudden calamities such as earthquakes, floods, locust infestations and similar unforeseen disasters; b) man-made emergencies like an input of refugees; and c) food scarcity conditions caused by crop failures, pests and diseases. The Emergency Food Reserve of 500,000 tons of grain, established by the General Assembly at its Seventh Special Session, was intended to strengthen the capacity of WFP to deal with emergency situations outside the normal natural disaster needs. In addition to emergency assistance, over 75 percent of WFP development aid during 1975 and the first four months of 1976 was for projects in the most seriously affected and least developed countries. There are no specific provisions for special assistance for economic emergencies, but it is assumed that this type of situation would fall into one of the previously defined categories for assistance.

SUMMARY

At the outset of this discussion, the question was posed as to whether or not the present United Nations arrangements contribute to or hinder increased involvement in disaster preparedness. Since 1972, better management procedures have evolved which have made the use of United Nations resources for disaster relief more effective. It must be understood that

while some international disaster relief will always be needed,
relief is basically a short-term approach to poverty in the
developing world - a treatment of the symptoms and not of the
cause of the problem.   Until such time that poor countries,
which are vulnerable to disaster, can develop sufficient resources for preventing natural disasters, the United Nations
should at least help them develop their own resources to deal
with disasters which are inevitable.

Despite its reputation and wide experience over the years
in international disaster relief, the United Nations cannot
maintain its position of leadership without adapting to new
conditions.   The growing involvement of other governments
and international agencies in disaster relief and preparedness,
the growing concern of the developing world about the effect
of disasters on economic and social development, and the
changing views of disaster relief as charity, are trends to
which the United Nations must respond.   The growing scale
and complexity of disaster relief demands greater profes-
sionalism in pre-disaster planning on the part of the United
Nations agencies.   Closer cooperation not only within the
United Nations, but also with other governments and agencies
involved in disaster preparedness programs will help to integrate the United Nations approach to preparedness, prevent
duplication of effort, and increase the chances of the developing world to survive the devastation that natural disasters
can bring.

5 Prospects for the Future

Natural disasters are not isolated incidents, but development problems requiring planned, coordinated and long-term responses. While some disaster relief is necessary, relief should not remain the only United Nations strategy for combating disaster. Greater attention should be paid to disaster preparedness and disaster prevention programs.

This research has reviewed the potential benefits and some of the problems involved in formulating national disaster preparedness plans in disaster-prone developing countries. The 49 least developed and most seriously affected countries have been identified as vulnerable to natural disasters. These countries are unable to raise the necessary resources to combat this problem. While some of these countries have received technical advice from several United Nations organizations, very little has been done to transfer this advice into operational preparedness programs. Other countries are lacking even the most rudimentary form of disaster plan and organization.

Disaster-prone developing countries have many different needs in disaster preparedness. They include vulnerability analysis, prediction and warning systems, educational and training programs, administrative support to create disaster legislation and a national relief organization. A key element in a country's disaster preparedness is a plan which specifies how the available human and natural resources will be mobilized in case of a disaster relief operation. However, the governments of disaster-prone developing countries must decide for themselves what is a reasonable level of preparedness in view of the overall development priorities and stages of development. The United Nations can assist in this assessment and help these countries institute greater measures of disaster preparedness.

There are many potential benefits in applying scientific and technical knowledge to prevent, prepare for, and assist in mitigating the effects of disasters. At the present time, however, there is a significant gap between technological development and the utilization of technology to address the problems of disasters. Few systems have been specifically designed for controlling the effects of disasters. Therefore, these systems must be adapted in order to be useful. This adaptation becomes difficult because there is little standardization or comparability among different systems. Finally, utilizing sophisticated technology requires a level of technical management that is usually scarce in developing countries. The United Nations can play a vital role in assisting disaster-prone governments in applying and adapting the available scientific and technical knowledge, and that which will be developed in the future, to the problems of natural disasters.

This study has also examined the provisions for disaster relief assistance of the major United Nations donors, as well as the activities of UNDRO as the coordinator of these operations. The current availability of United Nations resources for disaster preparedness activities has been assessed and recommendations made for increased involvement.

There are a number of problems that hinder most of the agencies and prevent them from instituting more of these programs in the developing countries. The foremost of these problems is a lack of a comprehensive system-wide United Nations strategy for disaster preparedness. In 1974, the Secretary-General identified in his report to the Economic and Social Council some of the elements of a United Nations program for preparedness and prevention. He suggested technical surveys, studies, the identification of specific projects in individual developing countries, and an allocation of funds for pre-disaster planning which would normally be earmarked for development purposes. UNDRO has conducted technical surveys and studies and will probably continue, in the future, to approach the subject of preparedness in this way. The remainder of this program, as identified by the Secretary-General, as yet has not been realized.

This lack of a stated policy, either in the form of guidelines from UNDRO, an international conference decision or a General Assembly resolution, has left organizations like FAO, WFP, WHO, UNDP and UNICEF without guidance as to their responsibilities and scope of action. Before any further action can be taken on this subject there must be a policy defined on what types of activities the United Nations will promote and what organization will direct and coordinate this activity. This policy must ensure that the objectives of disaster preparedness programs complement and are integrated with the overall development goals of the countries concerned, and that provisions are made for this coordination. Further, a United

Nations strategy for disaster preparedness should make provisions for the financing and implementation of specific projects in order that preparedness should not remain an advisory service, but become an operational program of development.

There are at least three important aspects of UNDRO's mandate which make it imperative that UNDRO be involved in articulating and coordinating the United Nations disaster preparedness strategy. UNDRO was directed to "mobilize, direct and co-ordinate" relief activities. This directive places UNDRO, of all the United Nations organizations involved in disaster relief, in a central position to assess some of the problems to be resolved by disaster preparedness plans. A second aspect of the mandate concerns UNDRO's responsibility to work out agreements with other United Nations organizations regarding their respective responsibilities. The Disaster Relief Coordinator is in the best position to advise disaster-prone countries regarding the areas of United Nations competence in relief matters. Finally, and most importantly, Resolution 2816 (XXVI) gives UNDRO the mandate to provide advice to governments on pre-disaster planning and to draw upon the United Nations resources available for such programs.

UNDP also can play a very important role in defining the United Nations strategy for disaster preparedness. The UNDP Resident Representative, as the representative of UNDRO in the disaster-stricken country, is the agency in the best position to assist in the implementation of disaster preparedness programs. Governments which will be designing and carrying out these programs usually have close contact with this office in disaster-related matters. The UNDRO guidelines give the UNDP Resident Representative primary responsibility as a catalyst for bringing about increased governmental awareness of natural hazards and the benefits of pre-disaster planning. Disaster preparedness is a development problem and such programming should be integrated into the long-term development program of a country. UNDP is in the best position to fulfill this function. Finally, as the focal point for United Nations development assistance, UNDP has the capability of enlisting all the technical resources and expert manpower of the United Nations system of agencies to assist disaster-prone countries in realizing their preparedness goals.

Together, UNDRO and UNDP can create and spearhead a United Nations disaster preparedness strategy. A coordinated approach by all of the relevant agencies of the system will prevent omission of important aspects of preparedness programming and allow the United Nations to offer diversified services to those countries requesting assistance.

The suggestions proposed by this study for increased United Nations involvement in disaster preparedness are intended to provide a basis for discussion which will lead to a new policy of action.   In the face of repeated disasters of increasing severity, relief has proven to be an inadequate approach to the problems of developing countries.

Some areas of the developing world are becoming increasingly susceptible to natural disasters, because of population growth, and the concentration of humanity in disaster-prone areas.   It has been predicted that the disasters of the 1980s will produce catastrophes greater than any the world has previously known.   The seriousness of this situation demands that the United Nations take action to institute a program of preparedness for those countries requesting assistance.

In the decade ahead, the United Nations will be increasingly called upon to respond to the demands of natural disasters of growing magnitude and severity.   Resources for this activity are not unlimited and the United Nations must adopt a new policy of encouraging member states to prepare for disasters in advance.   This may be the only humane approach to resolving the problems of disaster relief in the developing world.

Appendix A: United Nations General Assembly, Twenty-seventh Session, 14 December 1971, Assistance in Cases of National Disasters and Other Disaster Situations* (A/RES/2816)

The General Assembly,

Bearing in mind that throughout history natural disasters and emergency situations have inflicted heavy loss of life and property, affecting every people and every country,

Aware of and concerned about the suffering caused by natural disasters and the serious economic and social consequences for all, especially the developing countries,

Also aware of the varying needs of nations experiencing such disorders, which present new challenges for international co-operation,

Concerned about the ability of the international community to come to the aid of countries in a disaster situation,

Recalling its resolutions 2034 (XX) of 7 December 1965, 2435 (XXIII) of 19 December 1968, 2608 (XXIV) of 16 December 1969 and 2717 (XXV) of 15 December 1970, and Economic and Social Council resolutions 1533 (XLIX) of 23 July 1970 and 1546 (XLIX) of 30 July 1970 on assistance in cases of natural disaster,

Expressing appreciation of the Secretary-General's comprehensive report and of its perceptive examination of all aspects of the question, and taking note of the relevant passage in his statement to the Economic and Social Council on 5 July 1971,

---

*Twenty-seventh session, December 14, 1971 (A/RES 2816).

Taking note of Economic and Social Council resolution 1612 (LI) of 23 July 1971 on assistance in cases of natural disaster and other emergency situations,

Noting the study, annexed to the Secretary-General's report, on the legal status of disaster relief units made available through the United Nations,

Mindful of the need to strengthen and make more effective the collective efforts of the international community, and particularly the United Nations system, in the field of international disaster assistance,

Bearing in mind that assistance provided at the request of the stricken countries, without prejudice to their individual country programmes under the United Nations Development Programme, can be an effective contribution to the rehabilitation and development of the stricken areas,

Bearing in mind also that the possible response of the International Bank for Reconstruction and Development and other credit organizations and development agencies to a request from the Governments concerned for complementary assistance to the stricken areas, without prejudice to the assistance provided by those organizations for the normal development programmes of the stricken countries, can be an important element in the reconstruction and development of those areas,

Noting the competence of the United Nations and its related agencies, the United Nations Children's Fund, the United Nations High Commissioner for Refugees and the World Food Programme to render assistance in cases of natural disaster situations,

Noting further the key role which the resident representatives of the United Nations Development Programme could play at the country level,

Recognizing the vital role in international relief played by the International Red Cross and other voluntary societies,

Recognizing further the necessity to ensure prompt, effective and efficient response to a Government's need for assistance, at the time of a natural disaster or other disaster situation, that will bring to bear the resources of the United Nations system, prospective donor countries and voluntary agencies,

1. Calls upon the Secretary-General to appoint a Disaster Relief Co-ordinator, who will be authorized, on his behalf:

(a) To establish and maintain the closest co-operation with all organizations concerned and to make all possible advance arrangements with them for the purpose of ensuring the most effective assistance;

(b) To mobilize, direct and co-ordinate the relief activities of the various organizations of the United Nations system's response to a request for disaster assistance from a stricken State;

(c)   To co-ordinate United Nations assistance with assistance given by inter-governmental and non-governmental
organizations, in particular by the International Red Cross;

(d)   To receive, on behalf of the Secretary-General,
contributions offered to him for disaster relief assistance to be
carried out by the United Nations, its agencies and programmes for particular emergency situations;

(e)   To assist the Government of the stricken country to
assess its relief and other needs and to evaluate the priority
of those needs, to disseminate that information to prospective
donors and others concerned, and to serve as a clearinghouse
for assistance extended or planned by all sources of external
aid;

(f)   To promote the study, prevention, control and
prediction of natural disasters, including the collection and
dissemination of information concerning technological developments;

(g)   To assist in providing advice to Governments on
pre-disaster planning in association with relevant voluntary
organizations, particularly with the League of Red Cross
Societies, and to draw upon United Nations resources available
for such purposes;

(h)   To acquire and disseminate information relevant to
planning and co-ordinating disaster relief, including the improvement and establishment of stockpiles in disaster-prone
areas, and to prepare suggestions to ensure the most effective
use of available resources;

(i)   To phase out relief operations under his aegis as the
stricken country moves into the stage of rehabilitation and
reconstruction, but to continue to interest himself, within the
framework of his responsibilities for relief, in the activities of
the United Nations agencies concerned with rehabilitation and
reconstruction;

(j)   To prepare an annual report for the Secretary-
General, to be submitted to the Economic and Social Council
and to the General Assembly;

2.   Recommends that the Disaster Relief Co-ordinator
should be appointed by the Secretary-General normally for a
term of five years and at a level comparable to that of an
Under-Secretary-General of the United Nations;

3.   Endorses the Secretary-General's proposals for an
adequate permanent office in the United Nations which shall be
the focal point in the United Nations system for disaster relief
matters;

4.   Recommends that the office should be headed by the
Disaster Relief Co-ordinator and located in Geneva, be a
distinct element within the United Nations Secretariat and be
augmented as necessary by short-term secondment of personnel
for individual emergencies;

5. Requests the Secretary-General to prepare for the Economic and Social Council at its fifty-third session, taking into account any relevant suggestions and the experience gained by the Disaster Relief Co-ordinator, a report on any further steps which may be required to enable the Disaster Relief Co-ordinator adequately to perform the functions entrusted to him under the present resolution;

6. Further endorses the plan for a roster of volunteers to be drawn from experienced staff members of the United Nations system and interested non-governmental organizations, who could be made available at very short notice;

7.. Recommends that the Disaster Relief Co-ordinator should maintain contact with the Governments of Member States of the United Nations or members of specialized agencies or of the International Atomic Energy Agency concerning available aid in emergency situations, such as food supplies, medicines, personnel, transportation and communications, as well as advice to countries in pre-disaster planning and preparedness;

8. Invites potential recipient Governments:

(a) To establish disaster contingency plans with appropriate assistance from the Disaster Relief Co-ordinator;

(b) To appoint a single national disaster relief co-ordinator to facilitate the receipt of international aid in times of emergency;

(c) To establish stockpiles of emergency supplies such as tents, blankets, medicines and non-perishable food-stuffs;

(d) To make necessary arrangements for the training of administrative and relief personnel;

(e) To consider appropriate legislative or other measures to facilitate the receipt of aid, including over-flight and landing rights and necessary privileges and immunities for relief units;

(f) To improve national disaster warning systems;

9. Invites potential donor Governments:

(a) To consider and to continue offering on a wider basis emergency assistance in disaster situations;

(b) To consider and to continue offering on a wider basis emergency assistance in disaster situations;

(c) To inform the Disaster Relief Co-ordinator in advance about the facilities and services they might be in a position to provide immediately, including where possible relief units, logistical support and means of effective communication;

10. Decides to authorize the Secretary-General to draw on the Working Capital Fund in the amount of $200,000 for emergency assistance in any one year, with a normal ceiling of $20,000 per country in the case of any one disaster;

11. Further invites all organizations of the United Nations system and all other organizations involved to co-operate with the Disaster Relief Co-ordinator.

2018th plenary meeting,
December 14, 1971.

Appendix B:
Index of United Nations Agencies Involved in Disaster-Related Activities*

1. Food and Agriculture Organization.
   The Office for Special Relief Operations (OSRO) provides agricultural production inputs and technical assistance. Relief measures for disasters with longer-term consequences, as in the case of drought, include recovery and rehabilitation. This office served as the United Nations focal point for disaster relief to the Sahel from 1973 to 1975.

2. Intergovernmental Committee for European Migration (ICEM),
   ICEM has agreed to act at UNDRO's request, and on its behalf, to arrange aircraft charters for relief supplies.

3. International Atomic Energy Agency (IAEA),
   IAEA assists UNDRO in conducting relief operations arising from a nuclear accident.

4. International Bank for Reconstruction and Development (IBRD), the International Development Association (IDA), and the International Finance Corporation (IFC).
   IBRD, IDA and IFC (The World Bank Group) is not authorized to provide assistance in cases of national disasters, but has given concessionary terms to countries requesting rehabilitation and reconstruction assistance following a disaster.

---

*For a more detailed account, see United Nations Environment Programme, "Review of the Priority Subject Area, Natural Disasters," Report of the Executive Director (Nairobi: UNEP, 1977), Appendix I.

5. International Labour Organisation (ILO).
    This organization participates in urgent relief em-
    ployment training measures and quick rehabilitation of
    damaged infrastructures.
6. International Telecommunication Union (ITU).
    ITU has completed a study concerning the use of
    space radio communications systems to aid in natural
    disasters.
7. Office of the United Nations Disaster Relief Coordinator
    (UNDRO).
    UNDRO's role is to mobilize and coordinate disaster
    relief, and to promote disaster prevention and prepared-
    ness. It serves as the United Nations focal point for all
    disaster relief operations.
8. United Nations Children's Fund (UNICEF).
    The Coordinator of Emergency Operations directs
    special emergency relief to mothers and children in a
    disaster-stricken area to combat hunger and malnutrition.
9. United Nations Development Programme (UNDP).
    UNDP is the major coordinating body for UN devel-
    opment assistance. Recognizing that disaster prepared-
    ness should be a vital consideration in development plan-
    ning, UNDRO and UNDP are planning increased assistance
    for national disaster preparedness projects.
10. United Nations Educational, Scientific and Cultural Or-
    ganization (UNESCO).
    UNESCO has no specific disaster-related program,
    but is conducting geophysical investigations of various
    natural disasters, natural hazards and their mitigation.
    The Division of Educational Policy, Planning and Ad-
    ministration is studying the construction of "disaster-
    proof" school buildings.
11. United Nations Environment Programme (UNEP).
    UNEP has become increasingly involved since 1974 in
    studies related to disaster prevention. It has supported
    a series of UNDRO studies and organized the Desert-
    ification Conference in August 1977. A joint program
    with WMO is being conducted to assist several cyclone-
    prone countries with their monitoring systems. The
    planned Global Environmental Monitoring System aims to
    monitor climatic changes, including natural disasters.
12. United Nations High Commissioner for Refugees (UNHCR).
    UNHCR served as the United Nations focal point for
    disaster relief to the East Bengali refugees in India
    (1971-72). When a refugee situation occurs as a result of
    some man-made disaster (civil disturbance, war, revolu-
    tion, etc.), UNHCR is usually involved.
13. United Nations Industrial Development Organisation
    (UNIDO).
    UNIDO cooperates with UNDRO in all fields which fall

within its technical competence to lessen the impact of
disasters, and to ensure that adequate disaster preparedness measures are planned for and implemented in
all types of industrial development projects located in
hazardous areas.

14. World Food Programme (WFP).
     The Emergency Unit within WFP assists disaster-
stricken countries in assessing their emergency requirements and coordinates multilateral and bilateral food
assistance.

15. World Health Organization (WHO).
     The main function of the Office of Emergency Relief
Operations within WHO is to coordinate the provision of
technical advice and assistance, and the procurement and
shipment of medical supplies to a disaster-stricken area.

16. World Meteorological Organization (WMO).
     WMO is collaborating with UNDRO and UNEP on a
disaster prevention and mitigation study and has several
programs which are related to weather-related disaster
forecasting and warning.

Appendix C:
UNDRO Technical
Advisory Missions

Disaster Preparedness	Dates
1. Afghanistan (3)	August 1973
	August 1974
	April-October 1976
2. Malagasy Republic	December 1973-February 1974
3. Algeria	December 1973-March 1974
Tunisia	
Morocco	
4. Pakistan (2)	June-September 1974
	October-December 1974
5. Bolivia	July-October 1974
6. Guatemala	August-November 1975
7. El Salvador	August-November 1975
8. Honduras	August-November 1975
9. Turkey (2)	June-September 1974
	October 3-7, 1976
10. Indonesia	February-August 1975
11. Yemen	December 1975-May 1976
12. Morocco	January-February 1976
13. Sudan	November 1976-February 1977
14. Bangladesh	August 1976
15. Egypt	October 1976-March 1977
16. Dominican Republic	September-December 1976
17. Greece	March-April 1977

Disaster Prevention	Dates
1. Philippines	October 1976-February 1977
2. Yemen	August 1976
3. Nepal	April 1977

112

Appendix D:
State of
Disaster Preparedness
in the Poorest of
Developing Countries

Country	Potential Disaster Hazards (in order of importance)	National Disaster Organization	National Disaster Plan
Afghanistan	Flood, drought, earthquake, epidemic	Office of Emergency Preparedness	As of 1973, there is a new plan under discussion. Voluntary fund of AFS one million
Bangladesh	Cyclone, tidal bore, flood, epidemics, drought	Ministry of Relief and Rehabilitation	The Ministry of Relief and Rehabilitation is a permanent relief organization responsible coordinating relief activities of the government and of international and voluntary agencies and of bilateral donors. In actuality, the Bangladesh Red Cross carries out many warning and relief operations, particularly in the case of cyclones. Twenty-four million take (US$300,000.00) recurring cost for one year provided by government for Red Cross program

Country	Potential Disaster Hazards (in order of importance)	National Disaster Organization	National Disaster Plan
Benin	NA*	No permanent organization; ad hoc committees set up for each disaster	No plan exists
Bhutan	NA	NA	NA
Botswana	NA	No permanent organization	The police are charged with the control and coordination of disaster assistance
Burma	Cyclone, storm, flood	Ministry of Social Welfare, Dept. of Relief and Re-settlement	None; ad hoc control centers
Burundi	NA	No permanent organization	No plan exists
Cameroon	NA	No permanent organization	No plan exists
Cape Verde	NA	NA	NA
Central African Empire	NA	No permanent organization; ad hoc committee was set up after flood in September 1973	No plan exists

*NA: not available.

Country	Potential Disaster Hazards (in order of importance)	National Disaster Organization	National Disaster Plan
Chad	Drought, famine, epidemic,	Agency for the Defense Against Natural Calamities (DLCEN)	No national plan exists
Egypt	NA	No permanent organization; various government services are involved	A plan exists under the authority the General Administrative Office for Social Security and Relief
El Salvador	NA	National Emergency Committee	A plan exists
Ethiopia	Drought, epidemic	Relief and Rehabilitation Commission	Composed of various ministries and organizations. Responsible for relief and rehabilitation
Gambia	NA	No permanent organization	A plan exists
Ghana	NA	No permanent organization	No plan exists
Guinea	NA	No permanent organization	No plan exists
Guinea Bissau	NA	NA	NA

Country	Potential Disaster Hazards (in order of importance)	National Disaster Organization	National Disaster Plan
Guyana	NA	No permanent organization	No national plan, but each division has a plan
Haiti	Hurricane, flood, fire, drought	No permanent organization; Haitian Red Cross is official relief organization	The National Disaster Plan was approved in 1976. The Haitian Red Cross president directs pre-disaster planning and relief oper-ations. Regional and local com-mittees have formed disaster teams which are preparing to assess local disasters, provide initial relief and report to a national committee
Honduras	NA	Permanent National Emergency Council (COPEN)	COPEN directs all disaster relief operations, establishes committees and work groups, and coordinates all private organization internation-al agency relief activities
India	Flood, storm, epidemic, drought	Central Emergency Relief	The Central Emergency Relief acts in an advisory and coordinating capacity. Its duties are to assess the magnitude of the disaster; coordinate the government's efforts in disasters; and provide relief aid. All functions of direction, planning and executive are vested in state governments and lower administrative bodies. Particular-ly disaster-prone regions have established disaster plans and or-ganizations with responsibilities assigned to army, police and pub-lic services
Ivory Coast	NA	NA	NA

Country	Potential Disaster Hazards (in order of importance)	National Disaster Organization	National Disaster Plan
Kampuchea, Democratic	NA	No permanent organization	No plan exists
Kenya	NA	No permanent national organization exists, but there are local disaster committees and a central ad hoc disaster committee	No plan exists
Laos	NA	A permanent organization exists but there is no further information available	A national disaster plan exists
Lesotho	NA	No permanent organization	No plan exists
Madagascar	Flood, storm, cyclone	National Relief Council	In 1972, the government set up a plan of organization of assistance in cases of cyclones. It provides for a National Relief Council composed of government services and private organizations chaired by the Ministry of the Interior and an executive general staff under the armed forces. Preparation against the cyclone season is the responsibility of local authorities. Disaster assistance is administered and coordinated by the National Relief Council

Country	Potential Disaster Hazards (in order of importance)	National Disaster Organization	National Disaster Plan
Malawi	NA	No permanent organization	No plan exists
Maldives	NA	No permanent organization	No plan exists
Mali	Drought, famine, epidemic	Sahel Disaster Relief Organization	No plan exists
Mauritania	Drought, famine, epidemic	No permanent organization	No plan exists
Mozambique	NA	NA	NA
Nepal	NA	Ad hoc committees but no permanent address	No plan exists
Niger	Drought, famine, epidemic	An interministerial committee is responsible for organizing and coordinating disaster assistance. Local committees have been set up in certain areas	No plan exists

Country	Potential Disaster Hazards (in order of importance)	National Disaster Organization	National Disaster Plan
Pakistan	Flood, earthquake, drought, epidemic, locust invasion, border conflict, landslide, tsunami	Disaster Relief Committee	Local UNDP coordinates foreign donor relief effort, reports to foreign donors and appeals for foreign assistance. Has flood control plan to be completed 1980-81. There is an improved warning system with weather radar and satellite stations. Disaster relief plans are underway at federal, provincial capital and district levels
Rwanda	NA	NA	NA
Senegal	NA	The National Foundation for Social Work is responsible for disaster assistance	No plan exists
Sierra Leone	NA	NA	NA
Sikkim	NA	NA	NA
Somalia	Drought, famine, epidemic	No permanent organization	No plan exists
Sri Lanka	NA	The Ministry of Social Affairs	The Ministry of Social Affairs is responsible for disaster relief and has formulated plans at all levels

Country	Potential Disaster Hazards (in order of importance)	National Disaster Organization	National Disaster Plan
Sudan	NA	NA	NA
Tanzania	NA	NA	NA
Uganda	NA	No permanent organization	No plan exists
Upper Volta	NA	NA	NA
Western Samoa	Hurricane, flood, earthquake, tsunami, volcanic eruption	No permanent organization	A national plan exists
Yemen, Arab Republic	NA	NA	NA
Yemen, People's Democratic Republic	NA	NA	NA

Notes

CHAPTER 1

1. New York Times, "60 are Killed by Earthquake in Southern Iran," Wednesday, March 23, 1977.
2. New York Times, "Prolonged Drought in Haiti Brings Thousands to Brink of Starvation," Tuesday, May 17, 1977.
3. Washington Post, "Freak Eruption of Volcano Kills 100 in Zaire," Wednesday, June 8, 1977.
4. New York Times, "India Begins Major Relief Effort As Cyclone Deaths Reach 10,000," Tuesday, November 22, 1977.
5. Joseph M. Segel, United States Mission to the United Nations, Press release, US UN 153 (74), October 30, 1974.
6. United Nations General Assembly, Twenty-eighth Session, December 14, 1973, Report of the Secretary-General Concerning the Implementation of General Assembly Resolution 2790 (XXVI) and Security Council Resolution 307 (1971) (A/8996/Add. 3, Annex 1).
7. Russell R. Dynes, "A Perspective on Disaster Planning," Disaster Research Center Report Series No. 11, Columbus: Ohio State University, June 1972.
8. United Nations Environment Program, "Review of the Priority Subject Area: Natural Disasters" (Nairobi: UNEP, 1977), p. 1.
9. Muriel Skeet, Manual for Disaster Relief Work (Edinburgh: Churchill Livingston, 1977), pp. 1-2.
10. K.W. Westgate and P. O'Keefe, "Some Definitions of Disaster," Occasional Paper No. 4, Disaster Research Unit, University of Bradford, Yorkshire, United Kingdom, June 1976.

11.   Nicole Ball, "The Myth of the Natural Disaster," The Ecologist 5 (December 1975): 368-371.
12.   Ibid.
13.   Stephen Green, International Disaster Relief: Toward A Responsive System (New York: McGraw-Hill, 1977).
14.   United Nations Association of the United States of America, Acts of Nature, Acts of Man: The Global Response to Natural Disasters (New York: United Nations Association, 1977), p. 15. These estimates are based upon the median variant estimates for global population growth for 1970 to 2000 made in 1973 by the United Nations Population Division of the Department of Economic and Social Affairs.
15.   New York Times, "UN Food Agency Says Few Gains Have Been Made Against Hunger," January 4, 1978.
16.   United Nations Association of the United States of America, p. 16.
17.   Office of the United Nations Disaster Relief Coordinator, "The Protection of Human Settlements from Natural Disasters" (Paper presented at the United Nations Conference on Human Settlements, Vancouver, Canada, May 31 - June 11, 1976, p. 3.
18.   Ibid, p. 4.
19.   Ibid, p. 5.

CHAPTER 2

1.   William Dalton, Office of Foreign Disaster Assistance, U.S. Department of State (Statement made to the International Disaster Preparedness Seminar, Washington, D.C., June 8, 1977).
2.   Richard Pordes, "The Funding of International Relief Assistance in Natural Disaster Situations," United Nations Association of the United States of America (Paper presented at Policy Studies Panel on International Disaster Relief, January 1977), Annex, Table 3.
3.   United Nations Environment Program, Review of the Priority Subject Area: National Disasters (Report of the Executive Director, 1977), p. 19.
4.   United Nations General Assembly Twenty-sixth session, December 14, 1971, Assistance in Cases of Natural Disaster and Other Disaster Situations (A/2816).
5.   Ibid.
6.   United Nations General Assembly, Thirty-first session, May 12, 1976, Office of the United Nations Disaster Relief Co-ordinator, Report of the Secretary-General (A/31/88), Annex; United Nations General Assembly, Thirty-second session, May 12, 1977, Office of the United Nations Disaster Relief Co-ordinator, Report of the Secretary-General (A/32/64), Annex I.

7. Barbara J. Brown, Janet C. Tuthill, and E. Thomas Rowe, "International Disaster Response: The Sahelian Experience," (Washington, D.C.: U.S. Department of State, June 1976).

8. Ibid, p. VA 3.

9. Ibid, p. VA 5.

10. David J. Holdsworth, "The Present Role of Red Cross in Assistance," Joint Committee for the Re-appraisal of the Role of the Red Cross, Background Paper No. 3 (Geneva: Henri Dunant Institute, 1975), p. 9.

11. Lars Nelson (Correspondent for Newsweek), statement to the International Disaster Preparedness Seminar, U.S. Department of State, Washington, D.C., July 8, 1977.

12. Brown, Tuthill and Rowe, "International Disaster Response," p. VA 9.

13. United Nations, Economic and Social Council, Fiftieth Session, 1971. Assistance in Cases of Natural Disaster, Comprehensive Report of the Secretary-General (E/4994), Annex IV.

14. Office of the United Nations Disaster Relief Coordinator, internal memorandum to the United Nations Disaster Relief Coordinator from the Legal Counsel concerning the competence of the Disaster Relief Coordinator June 9, 1972, pp. 7, 17.

15. United Nations, Economic and Social Council, Fiftieth Session (E/4994), p. 9.

16. United Nations General Assembly, Twenty-sixth Session, Third Committee, 1888th meeting, November 30, 1971, Assistance in Cases of Natural Disaster (A/C. 3/SR.1888).

17. Ellen Freudenheim, "A Study of the Types, Frequency and Importance of Political Problems Occurring in Natural Disaster Situations" (Paper prepared for UNA-USA Policy Studies Panel on International Disaster Relief, January 1977).

CHAPTER 3

1. Economic and Social Commission for Asia and the Pacific, the World Meteorological Organization and the League of Red Cross Societies, Guidelines for Disaster Prevention and Preparedness in Tropical Cyclone Areas (Geneva and Bangkok, 1977), p. 7.

2. Office of the United Nations Disaster Relief Coordinator, Guidelines for Disaster Prevention: Pre-disaster Physical Planning of Human Settlements, 1 (Geneva: UNDRO, 1976); Guidelines for Disaster Prevention: Building Measures for Minimizing the Impact of Disasters, 2 (Geneva:

UNDRO, 1976); Guidelines for Disaster Prevention: Management of Settlements, 3 (Geneva: UNDRO, 1976).

3.   Michel F. Lechat, "The Epidemiology of Disasters," Proceedings of the Royal Society of Medicine 69 (June 1976): 422.

4.   United Nations General Assembly, Twenty-fifth Session, December 16, 1970, International Cooperation in the Peaceful Uses of Outer Space (A/RES/27330).

5.   "Modernizing Our Methodology" editorial, The Hindu, November 30, 1977, p. 6.

6.   ESCAP/WHO LORCS, Guidelines, p. 85.

7.   Lechat, "The Epidemiology of Disasters," p. 421.

8.   G.N. Ritchie, "Disaster Preparedness," Journal of Administration Overseas (March 1977): 84.

9.   United Nations Economic and Social Council, Fifty-first session, Committee for Development Planning, Report on the Seventh Session, March 22 – April 1971 (E/4990); United Nations Special Fund, Board of Governors, Third Session, March 19, 1976, Current and Prospective Situation of the Developing Countries Most Seriously Affected by the Economic Crisis (UNSF/13).

10.   Ibid.

11.   For more detailed information on these programs, organizations, disaster hazards, and methods of funding relief operations for some of these countries see Appendix D.

CHAPTER 4

1.   Jean Mayer, "Emergency Priorities in Child Nutrition" (Report to the UNICEF Executive Board, May 1973).

2.   United Nations Childrens Fund, "Field Manual, Assistance Policies, Emergency Situation," vol. 1, book F, chap. 1, p. 14.

3.   Ibid, pp. 12-13.

4.   Ibid, p. 2.

5.   General Assembly Resolution 3250 (XXIX), December 1974.

6.   United Nations Association of the United States of America, Acts of Nature, Acts of Man: The Global Response to Natural Disasters (New York: United Nations Association, 1977), p. 16.

7.   For example, Barbara J. Brown, Janet C. Tuthill and E. Thomas Rowe, "International Disaster Response: The Sahelian Experience" (Washington, D.C.: U.S. Department of State, June 1976); Hal Sheets and Roger Morris, Disaster in the Desert (Washington, D.C.: The Carnegie Endowment for International Peace, 1974); Jack Shepherd,

The Politics of Starvation (Washington, D.C.: The Carnegie Endowment for International Peace, 1975).

8. United Nations, Economic and Social Council, Fourteenth Session, April 1952, Preparations for Famine Detection and Famine Emergency Relief Operations (E/425).

9. Food and Agriculture Organization, Council, Sixty-fifth Session, March 1975) (CL 65/Rep).

10. John Seaman (editorial), Disasters 1, no. 3 (1977): 169.

11. United Nations, Methodology of Nutritional Surveillance, Report of a Joint FAO/WHO/UNICEF Expert Committee, Technical Report Series, No. 593 (Geneva: WHO, 1976).

12. Compiled from World Food Programme, Ten Years of World Food Programme Development Aid 1963-1972 (Rome: FAO, 1973), p. 6.

13. World Food Programme/Intergovernmental Governing Council Resolution, 26/5-A (Rome, WFP, November 1974), p. 3.

14. An earlier report of 1963-72 activities estimated that 23 percent of WFP emergency operations were man-made (e.g., civil wars, border conflicts) (Ten Years of World Food Programme Development Aid, 1963-72) (Rome: WFP, 1973). No estimates are available for 1972-77 operations.

15. Ibid.

16. World Food Program/Committee on Food Aid 2/19, December 1976, pp. 4-5.

17. World Health Organization, World Health Assembly, First Session, July 1948 (WHA 1.61).

18. Twenty-fifth Session, World Health Organization, "WHO's Emergency Services in Epidemics" (Paper presented at the meeting on WHO and the Problems of Communicable Disease Control, November 28 - December 2, 1977, Geneva).

19. World Health Organization, World Health Assembly, Twenty-sixth Session, June 1973, (WHA 26.60); Twenty-seventh Session, May 1974 (WHA 27.48).

20. World Health Organization, World Health Asembly (WHA 27.48).

21. World Health Organization, World Health Assembly (WHA 28.45).

22. M.F. Lechat, "An Epidemiologists's View of Earthquakes," Engineering Seismology and Earthquake Engineering NATO, Advanced Studies Institute, Series E, Applied Sciences 3 (1974): 285-307.

23. Michel F. Lechat, "The Epidemiology of Disasters," Proceedings of the Royal Society of Medicine 69, no. 6 (June 1976): 424.

24. Karl A. Western, "Epidemiology of Communicable Disease in Disaster Situations" (Washington, D.C.: Pan American Health Organization, 1977), p. 2.

25.   C. de Ville de Goyet, et al. "Earthquake in Guatemala:
       Epidemiologic Evaluation of the Relief Effort," Bulletin of
       the Pan American Health Organization X, no. 2 (1976):
       103-104.
26.   Lechat, "Epidemiology of Disasters," pp. 424-425.
27.   Pan Ameican Health Organization, Directing Council,
       Twenty-fourth Meeting, October 1976, Tenth Resolution.
28.   C. de Ville de Goyet and M.F. Lechat, "Health Aspects
       in Natural Disasters," Tropical Doctor 6 (1976): 157.
29.   For example, E.K. Kroeger, "Disaster Manager in
       Tropical Countries," Tropical Doctor 6 (1976): 147-151.
30.   Karl A. Western, "The Epidemiology of Natural and
       Man-Made Disasters: The Present State of the Art"
       (Ph.D. diss., University of London, 1972), p. 86.
31.   Ibid., p. 81.
32.   C. de Ville de Goyet, E. Jeanee, M.F. Lechat, and A.
       Bouckaert, "Anthropometric Measurements in a Relief
       Programme in Niger: A Tool for Decision Making at the
       Community Level," Disasters 1, no. 3 (1977): 223-229.
33.   K. Hata, "Management Survey Report No. 137: Manage-
       ment Survey on Emergency Relief Operations" (Geneva:
       World Health Organization, October 1976).
34.   Ibid. p. 22.
35.   Ibid.
36.   Ibid. p. 20.
37.   Ibid. p. 21
38.   Ibid. p. 20
39.   United Nations General Asembly, Twenty-sixth Session,
       December 14, 1971, Assistance in Cases of Natural Disaster
       and Other Disaster Situations (A/RES/2816).
40.   United Nations General Assembly, Thirty-first Session,
       May 12 - June 1976, Office of the United Nations Disaster
       Relief Coordinator, Report of the Secretary General
       (A/31/88); Thirty-second Session, June 28, 1977,
       (A/32/64/Corr.1).
41.   For a complete account of the financial discussions see:
       United Nations General Assembly, Fifth Committee, Oc-
       tober 29, 1973, Provisional Summary Record of the 1582nd
       Meeting (A/C5/SR.1582); October 31, 1973, Provisional
       Summary Record of the 1586th Meeting (A/C5/SR.1587);
       November 2, 1973, Provisional Summary Record of the
       1587th Meeting (A/C5/SR.1587).
42.   United Nations General Assembly, Twenty-ninth session,
       June 5, 1974, Assistance in Cases of Natural Disaster and
       Other Disaster Situations (A/9637).
43.   Ibid.
44.   United Nations General Assembly, Twenty-ninth session,
       November 29, 1974, Strengthening of the Office of the
       United Nations Disaster Relief Co-ordinator (A/RES/3243).

45. United Nations General Assembly, Thirtieth Session, December 9, 1975, Assistance in Cases of Natural Disaster (A/RES/3440).

46. Agreements have been signed with the Food and Agriculture Organization (FAO), World Food Programme (WFP), United Nations Children's Fund (UNICEF), United Nations Environmental Program (UNEP), International Labour Organisation (ILO), International Atomic Energy Agency (IAEA), Intergovernmental Committee for European Migration (ICEM) and the United Nations Industrial Development Organisation (UNIDO).

47. United Nations General Assembly, Twenty-sixth Session (A/RES/2816).

48. United Nations General Assembly, Twenty-seventh Session, December 12, 1972, Assistance in Cases of Natural Disaster (A/RES/2959).

49. United Nations General Assembly, Twenty-eighth Session, December 14, 1973, Assistance in Cases of Natural Disaster (A/RES/3152).

50. United Nations General Assembly, Thirtieth Session (A/RES/3440).

51. United Nations General Assembly, Twenty-ninth Session (A/9637), p. 4.

52. Office of the United Nations Disaster Relief Coordinator, UNDRO Newsletter 1, no. 1 (August 1976): 6.

53. Ibid., p. 8.

54. Office of the United Nations Disaster Relief Coordinator, Disaster Prevention and Mitigation: Volcanological Aspects, vol. 1 (Geneva: UNDRO, 1976); Hydrological Aspects, vol. 2 (Geneva: UNDRO, 1977); Seismological Aspects, vol. 3; Meteorological Aspects, vol. 4; Land Use Aspects, vol. 5.

55. Office of the United Nations Disaster Relief Coordinator, Guidelines for Disaster Prevention: Pre-Disaster Physical Planning of Human Settlements, vol. 1 (Geneva: UNDRO, 1976); Building Measures for Minimizing Impact of Disasters, vol. 2; Management of Settlements, vol. 3.

56. United Nations General Assembly, Twenty-sixth Session (A/RES/2816).

57. United Nations General Assembly, Thirty-first Session, Report of UNDRO (A/31/88).

58. United Nations General Assembly, Twenty-eighth session (A/RES/3152).

59. United Nations General Assembly, Twentieth Session (A/9637), p. 3.

60. Ibid., p. 5.

61. United Nations General Assembly, Twenty-sixth Session (A/RES/2816).

62. United Nations Development Programme, August 26, 1975, Role of Resident Representative in Respect of Pre-Disaster Planning and Disaster Relief (UNDP/PROG/FIELD/58).

63. Ibid.
64. Margaret J. Anstee, Assistant Administrator, UNDP, "Disaster Relief," (Speech delivered before the UNA-USA Biennial Convention).
65. Ibid.
66. United Nations Economic and Social Council, Forty-eighth Session, April 28, 1970, The Role of The Co-operative Movement in the Achievement of the Goals and Objectives of the Second United Nations Development Decade (E/4807/Corr.1).
67. International Labour Organisation, Governing Body, 204th Session, November 1977, "Memorandum of Understanding Between the Director-General of the International Labour Organisation and the United Nations Disaster Relief Co-ordinator" (G.B. 204/10/6/1), Appendix.
68. International Labour Organisation, "Inter-Regional Project for Planning and Administration of Special Public Works Schemes: Training Course No. III: Project Design, Implementation and Evaluation" (Geneva: March 1977), part 1, section II, p. 6.
69. United Nations General Asssembly, Twenty-sixth Session (A/RES/2816).
70. Official Records of the Economic and Social Council, Fifty-seventh Session, summary records of plenary meetings, paras. 60-66, and Official Records of the General Assembly, Thirtieth Session, Supplement No. A (A/10003/Add.1), Annex IV; Paper submitted by the Delegation of Netherlands; United Nations General Assembly, Sixth Special Session, May 1974, Programmes of Action on the Establishment of a New International Economic Order (A/3202-5-VI).
71. United Nations General Assembly, Twenty-fifth Session, October 24, 1970, International Development Strategy for the United Nations (A/RES/2626).
72. United Nations Economic and Social Council, Sixty-first Session, July 22, 1976, Immediate Needs Resulting From Economic Emergency Situations (E/5843).
73. United Nations Economic and Social Council, Sixty-third Session, June 8, 1977, Immediate Needs Resulting from Economic Emergency Situations (E/5989).
74. Ibid.
75. United Nations Economic and Social Council, Sixty-first Session (E/5843), p. 5.
76. Ibid.
77. United Nations Conference on Trade and Development, Fourth Session, May 31, 1976, Least Developed Countries, Island Developing Countries and Land-locked Developing Countries (TD/RES/98).
78. United Nations Conference on Trade and Development, Fourth Session, May 31, 1976, Economic Situation in the Comoros (TD/RES/99).

79.   United Nations Economic and Social Council, Sixty-first
       Session (E/5843) Annex, p. 6.
80.   United Nations World Food Programme, Intergovernmental
       Committee, Seventeenth Session, March 1970 (WFP/IGC:
       17/5, Rev. 1).

Bibliography

BOOKS

Baker, George W., and Chapman, Dwight W., eds. Man and Society in Disaster. New York: Basic Books, 1962.

Barton, Allen H. Communities in Disaster. Garden City: Doubleday, 1969.

Blix, Gunnar; Hofvander, Yngue; and Vahlquist, Bo. Famine: Nutrition and Relief Operations in Times of Disaster. Uppsala, Sweden: Almquist and Wiksells, 1971.

Bower, Michael; Freeman, Gary; Miller, Kay; and Morris, Roger. Passing By: The United States and Genocide in Burundi, 1972. Washington, D.C: Carnegie Endowment, 1973.

Brown, Barbara J. "Dimensions of International Disaster Relief: An Overview of the Structure of the Current System." In The Global Response to Natural Disasters, edited by Lynn Stephens and Stephen Green. New York: New York University Press, 1978, forthcoming.

Dacy, Douglas C., and Kunreuther, Howard. The Economics of Natural Disaster. New York: National Academy of Sciences, 1958.

Davis, Morris, Civil Wars and the Politics of International Relief. New York: Praeger, 1975.

El-Khawas, Mohamed. "A Reassessment of International Relief Programs." In The Politics of Natural Disaster, edited by Michael H. Glantz, pp. 77-100. New York: Praeger, 1976.

Form, William H., and Nosow, Sigmund. Community in Disaster. New York: Harper and Brothers, 1958.

Glantz, Michael H. The Politics of Natural Disaster. New York: Praeger, 1976.

Hance, William A. "Lessons to be Learned from the Sahel Drought." In Africa: from Mystery to Maze, edited by Helen Kitchen, pp. 135-166. Lexington, Mass.: Lexington Books, 1976.

Imperato, P.J. "Health Care Systems in the Sahel: Before and After the Drought." In The Politics of Natural Disaster, edited by Michael H. Glantz, pp. 282-302. New York: Praeger, 1976.

Lillich, Richard B. "Humanitarian Assistance and Intervention: An Introduction." In The United Nations: A Reassessment - Sanctions, Peacekeeping and Humanitarian Assistance, edited by John M. Paxman and George T. Boggs, pp. 103-104. Charlottesville: University of Virginia Press, 1973.

Masefield, G.B. Food and Nutrition Procedures in Times of Disaster. Rome: FAO Nutritional Studies No. 21, 1967.

Raker, J.W.; Wallace, A.F.C.; Rayner, Jeanette F.; and Eckert, A.W. Emergency Medical Care in Disasters: A Summary of Recorded Experience. Washington, D.C.: National Academy of Sciences, 1956.

Salzberg, John. "The United Nations and the Bangladesh Crises: A Case Study of UN Capability to Deal with Massive Violations of Human Rights." In The United Nations: A Reassessment - Sanctions, Peacekeeping and Humanitarian Assistance, edited by John M. Paxman and George T. Boggs, pp. 114-128. Charlottesville: University of Virginia Press, 1973.

Scholt, Stephen C. "United States Relief to Civilian Victims of the Biafra-Nigerian War." In The United Nations: A Reassessment - Sanctions, Peacekeeping and Humanitarian Assistance, edited by John M. Paxman and George T. Boggs, pp. 105-113. Charlottesville: University of Virginia Press, 1973.

Sheets, Hal, and Morris, Roger. Disaster in the Desert: Failures in International Relief in the West African Drought. Washington, D.C.: Carnegie Endowment for International Peace, 1975.

Shepherd, Jack. The Politics of Starvation. Washington, D.C.: Carnegie Endowment for International Peace, 1975.

Skeet, Muriel. Manual for Disaster Relief Work. Edinburgh: Churchill Livingstone, 1977.

Tarakchandra, Das. Bengal Famine. Calcutta: University of Calcutta, 1949.

BIBLIOGRAPHY   133

Thompson, J.D., and Hawkes, R.W. "Disaster, Community
Organization and Administrative Process." In Man and Society
in Disaster, edited by George W. Baker and Dwight W.
Chapman, pp. 268-300. New York: Basic Books, 1962.

Tusharkanti, Shosh. The Bengal Tragedy. Lahore, India:
Hero Publications, 1944.

White, Gilbert F. Assessment of Research on Natural Hazards.
Cambridge: Massachusetts Institute of Technology Press, 1975.

ARTICLES IN JOURNALS

Aall, C. "Relief, Nutrition and Health Problems in the
Nigerian/Biafran War." Monograph #9. Journal of Tropical
Pediatrics 16 (1970):69.

Aaronson, Steve. "The Social Cost of Earthquake Prediction."
New Scientist 73 (March 1977):634-636.

Anderson, William A. "Social Structure and the Role of the
Military in Natural Disaster." Sociology and Social Research 53
(January 1969):242-253.

Brown, Barbara J. "The United Nations and Disaster Relief in
the Sahel, 1973-1975." Disasters: The International Journal
of Disaster Studies and Practice I, no. 2 (March 1977):145-150.

_____. "NGO/UN Interaction in Sahelian Disaster Relief,
1973-75," Transnational Associations, forthcoming.

Brown, R.K. "Disaster Medicine: What is it? Can it be
taught?" Journal of the American Medical Association 197
(1966):1081.

Burley, Lawrence A. "Disaster Relief Administration in the
Third World." International Development Review 15 (1973):8-
12.

_____. "Disaster Relief Administration in the Third World."
Development Digest 12 (1974):127-140.

de Ville de Goyet, C., and Lechat M.F. "Health Aspects in
Natural Disasters." Tropical Doctor 6 (1976):152-157.

de Ville de Goyet, C.; del Cid, Romero, A.; Jeannee, E.; and
Lechat, M.F. "Earthquake in Guatemala: Epidemiologic Evalu-
ation of the Relief Effort." Bulletin of the Pan American
Health Organization X, no. 2 (1976):95-109.

de Ville de Goyet, C.; Lechat, M.F.; and Boucquey, C.
"Drugs and Supplies for Disaster Relief." Tropical Doctor 6
(October 1976):168-170.

Fitzpatrick, J. "The Role of Emergency Grain Reserves in Developing Countries." Disasters I, no. 3 (1977):217-222.

Gilbert, J.E. "Human Behavior Under Conditions of Disaster." Medical Service Journal 14 (May 1958):318-324.

Gottlieb, Gideon. "International Assistance to Civilian Populations in Armed Conflicts." Journal of International Law and Politics 4 (1971):403.

_____. "The United Nations and Emergency Humanitarian Assistance in India-Pakistan." American Journal of International Law 66 (1972):362.

Hagen, Toni. "Problems of International Emergency Aid." Development Digest 12 (1974):122-124.

Heffron, Edward. "Interagency Relationships and Conflict in Disaster. The Wilkes-Barre Experience." Mass Emergencies 2, no. 2 (June 1977):111-120.

Imperato, P.J. "The Strategy and Tactic for Vaccinating the Population of the Inland Deltas of the Niger." Afrique Medicale 14 (1975):307-316.

Kroeger, E.K. "Disaster Management in Tropical Countries," Tropical Doctor 6 (October 1976):147-151.

Lechat, Michel F. Editorial. Tropical Doctor 6 (October 1976):145-146.

_____. "The Epidemiology of Disasters." Proceedings of the Royal Society of Medicine 69, no. 6 (June 1976):421-426.

McClure, Russell S. "Co-ordination of International Emergency Disaster Relief." Development Digest 12, no. 2 (1974):119-121.

Miller, J.P. "Medical Relief in the Nigerian Civil War." Lancet 1 (1970):1330.

Olson, Robert A., and Olson, Richard S. "The Guatemala Earthquake of 4 February 1976: Social Science Observations and Research." Mass Emergencies 2, no. 2 (June 1977):69-82.

"Predicting Famine." Editorial. Disasters 1, no. 3 (1977):167-168.

Quarantelli, E.L. "The Community General Hospital: Its Immediate Problems in Disasters." American Behavioral Scientist 13 (1970):380.

Roy, A.D. "The Organization of Medical Services for Disaster in a Tropical Country." Tropical Doctor 6 (1976):158-162.

Samuels, J.W. "Humanitarian Relief in Man-Made Disasters: The International Red Cross and the Nigerian Experience." Behind the Headlines 34, no. 3 (1975).

REPORTS

Assar, M. Guide to Sanitation in Natural Disasters. Geneva: WHO, 1971).

Brown, Barbara J.; Tuthill, Janet C.; Rowe, E. Thomas. "International Disaster Response: The Sahelian Experience." Washington, D.C.: U.S. Department of State, June 1976.

Economic and Social Commission for Asia and the Pacific and World Meteorological Organization, Report of the Regional Seminar on Community Preparedness and Disaster Prevention, November 23-29, 1976, Manila (WRD/TC. 9/9).

Hata, K. "Management Survey Report #137: Management Survey on Emergency Relief Operations." Geneva: WHO, October 1976.

Holdsworth, David J. "The Present Role of the Red Cross in Assistance," Joint Committee for the Re-appraisal of the Role of the Red Cross, Background Paper No. 3. Geneva: Henri Dunant Institute, 1975.

International Red Cross, Board of Governors, Thirty-fourth Session, October 7-11, 1977, Report of the First Asian Regional Red Cross Conference. New Delhi, March 1977 (CGL/21/1).

Krimgold, Frederick. "Pre-Disaster Planning. The Role of International Aid for Pre-disaster Planning in Developing Countries." Stockholm: Avdelningen for Arkitektur, KTH, 1974.

League of Red Cross Societies, Red Cross Disaster Relief Handbook. Geneva: League of Red Cross Societies, 1976.

Lewis, J.; O'Keefe, P.; and Westgate, A. "A Philosophy of Planning." Occasional Paper No. 5, University of Bradford Disaster Research Unit, 1977.

Meyer, Jean. UNICEF Assistance in Emergencies. Cambridge: Harvard School of Public Health, 1975.

Office of the United Nations Disaster Relief Coordinator. Disaster Prevention and Mitigation: Volcanological Aspects, Vol. 1. Geneva: UNDRO, 1976.

_____. Disaster Prevention and Mitigation, Hydrological Aspects. Vol. 2. Geneva: UNDRO, 1977.

_____. Disaster Prevention and Mitigation, Seismological Aspects. Vol. 3. Geneva: UNDRO, 1977.

_____. Disaster Prevention and Mitigation, Meteorological Aspects. Vol. 4. Geneva: UNDRO, 1977.

_____. Disaster Prevention and Mitigation, Land Use Aspects.
Vol. 5. Geneva: UNDRO, 1977.

_____.   Guidelines for Disaster Prevention, Pre-Disaster
Physical Planning of Human Settlements.   Vol. 1.   Geneva:
UNDRO, 1976.

_____. Guidelines for Disaster Prevention, Building Measures
for Minimizing the Impact of Disasters.   Vol. 2.   Geneva:
UNDRO, 1976.

_____.   Guidelines for Disaster Prevention, Management of
Settlements. Vol. 3. Geneva: UNDRO, 1976

_____.   "The Organization of Emergency Relief in Afghan-
istan." Geneva: UNDRO, 1976.

_____.   "La Movilizacion y Coordinacion de los Socorros en
Dasos de Desastre en la Republica Dominicana."   Geneva:
UNDRO, 1976.

_____. "Metro Manila Urban Master Plan: A Methodology for
Composite Vulnerability Analysis Associated with Natural Disaster Risks." Geneva: UNDRO, 1977.

Office of the United Nations High Commissioner for Refugees
Report. "A Story of Anguish and Action. The United Nations
Focal Point for Assistance to Refugees from East Bengal in
India." Geneva: UNHCR, November 1972.

Sav, G. Thomas.   "Natural Disasters: Some Empirical and
Economic Considerations."   Washington, D.C.: U.S. Department of Commerce, 1974.

Soliman, F.   "Health Protection in Emergency with Special
Reference to the Condition of Women and Children."   Mimeographed. Geneva: WHO, 1974.

Soliman, F.   "WHO's Role in Emergency Relief Operations."
Mimeographed. Geneva: WHO, July 25, 1974.

United Nations Association of the United States of America.
Acts of Nature, Acts of Man: The Global Response to Natural
Disasters. New York: UNA-USA, 1977.

United Nations Economic and Social Council. The Role of
Technology in Reducing the Impact of Natural Disasters on
Mankind. New York: United Nations, 1972.

United Nations World Food Programme. Ten Years of World
Food Programme Development Aid: 1963-1972.   Rome: FAO,
1973.

United States Department of State, General Accounting Office.
"Need to Build an International Disaster Relief Agency."
Comptroller-General's Report to the Congress. Washington,
D.C.: Department of State, September 1975.

United States Government. "Disaster Preparedness." Report
to the Congress. Washington, D.C.: 1972.

UNPUBLISHED MATERIALS

Brown, Barbara J. "Transnational Activity in Disaster Relief:
NGO/UN Interaction in the Sahel, 1973-1975." Paper presented
to the International Studies Association, West Conference, in
San Francisco, March 18-20, 1976.

Freudenheim, Ellen. "A Study of the Types, Frequency and
Importance of Political Problems Occurring in Natural Disaster
Situations, 1972-1976." Paper prepared for the United Nations
Association of the United States of America Policy Studies
Panel of International Disaster Relief, January 1977.

Green, Stephen. "The Role of the United Nations in Assistance to National Disaster Preparedness and Prevention Programmes." Paper prepared for the United Nations Association
of the United States of America Policy Studies Panel of International Disaster Relief, January 1977.

Hilda, T.M. "National Emergency Services in Papua New
Guinea." Statement to the International Disaster Preparedness
Seminar, Washington, D.C., June-July 1977.

Isenman, Paul J. and Singer, H.W. "Food Aid: Disincentives
and Their Policy Implications." Brighton, England: Institute
of Development Studies, University of Sussex, 1975.

Kroeger, E. "International Assistance in Natural Disasters:
Experiences and Proposals." Ph.D. dissertation, London
School of Hygiene and Tropical Medicine, University of
London, 1971.

Love, Lee and Cowlan, Bert. "Applications of Technology to
Disaster Relief." Paper prepared for the United Nations Association of the United States of America Policy Studies Panel
of International Disaster Relief, January 1977.

Ngah, Kamaruddin Bin. "Natural Disaster Preparation, Relief
and Rehabilitation Measures in Malaysia." Statement to the
International Disaster Preparedness Seminar, Washington,
D.C., June-July 1977.

Office of the United Nations Disaster Relief Coordinator. "The
Protection of Human Settlements from Natural Disasters. Paper
Prepared for Economic Co-operation." Statement to the Inter-
national Disaster Preparedness Seminar, Washington, D.C.,
June-July 1977.

Osborne, Robert. "Regional Organizations' Role in Disaster Preparedness and Relief Strategy: The Role of the South Pacific Bureau for Economic Co-operation." Statement to the International Disaster Preparedness Seminar, Washington, D.C., June-July 1977.

Palu, Tevita, Vainga. "Informal Comments on Tonga's National Disaster Plan." Statement to the International Preparedness Disaster Seminar, Washington, D.C., June-July 1977.

Pordes, Richard. "The Funding of International Relief Assistance in Natural Disaster Situations." Paper prepared for the United Nations Association of the United States of America Policy Studies Panel of International Disaster Relief, January 1977.

Rashid, Abdur. "Short Term Disaster Plan for Flood of the Government of the Peoples Republic of Bangladesh." Statement to the International Disaster Preparedness Seminar, Washington, D.C., June-July 1977.

Stephens, Lynn. "An Examination of Various Non-Formalistic Approaches to the Political Problems Associated with Natural Disasters." Paper prepared for the United Nations Association of the United States of America Policy Studies Panel of International Disaster Relief, January 1977.

Sumadinata, Andany. "The Handling of Natural Disaster in West Java." Statement to the International Disaster Preparedness Seminar, Washington, D.C., July 1977.

Weiler, Jack Meredith. "Innovations in Anticipation of Crises: Organizational Preparedness for Natural Disasters and Civil Disturbances." Ph.D. dissertation, Ohio State University, 1971.

Western, Karl A., M.D. "The Epidemiology of Natural and Man-Made Disasters: The Present State of the Art." Dissertation DTPH, University of London, 1972.

Zwingeberg, Linda, and Cowlan, Bert. "Some Background and Thoughts on International Disaster Relief Delivery Practices and Technology." Paper prepared for the United Nations Association of the United States of America Policy Studies Panel of International Disaster Relief, January 1977.

FILM

Space Between The Worlds: Diplomacy. Roger Graef, Producer. Film Prepared by the BCC in cooperation with KCET-TV, Los Angeles, July 1971. U.S. Department of State Library.

Index

Advisory Committee on Administration and Budgetary Questions (ACABQ), 77

Africa
disasters in, 9
death due to, 9
relief operations for, 8
economic emergencies in, 98
measles and smallpox in, 13

American
Central
disaster deaths in, 9
UNDP/UNDRO/ECLA
vulnerability study
of, 87
Latin
disasters in,
deaths due to, 9
incidence of, 68
relief operations for, 8
North
disaster deaths in, 9
South
disaster deaths in, 9

Angola
relief operations in, 17

Asia
disasters in,
deaths due to, 9
relief operations for, 8

Australasia
disaster deaths in, 9

Australia
disaster preparedness in, 43, 44

Bangladesh
Bay of Bengal cyclone in, 6, 36-7, 37
civil war in, 67
disaster relief operations, 6, 64
East Bengali refugee relief operations, 17

Caribbean
disasters in
deaths due to, 9
incidence of, 68
relief operations for, 8

Catholic Relief Services (CRS), 22
See also Voluntary Agencies

Central America
disasters in
deaths due to, 9
UNDP/UNDRO/ECLA
vulnerability study
of ,87
See also America.

139

About the Author

Barbara Brown (PhD - University of Denver), formerly research associate with UNITAR, is with Development Alternatives, Inc., a Washington consulting firm. She has also worked for the World Bank. Dr. Brown has contributed to Disasters Journal, as well as to the book Disaster Assistance: Appraisal, Reform, and New Approaches.

Pergamon Policy Studies